INVICTUS

INVICTUS

THE JUNGLE THAT MADE ME

Nidhie Sharma

PAN

First published 2021 by Pan
an imprint of Pan Macmillan Publishing India Private Limited
707, Kailash Building
26 K. G. Marg, New Delhi – 110 001
www.panmacmillan.co.in

Pan Macmillan, The Smithson, 6 Briset Street, London EC1M 5NR
Associated companies throughout the world
www.panmacmillan.com

ISBN 978-93-90742-07-3

1 3 5 7 9 8 6 4 2

Typeset in Adobe Garamond Pro by R. Ajith Kumar, New Delhi
Printed and bound in India by Replika Press Pvt. Ltd.

To my father,

your indomitable spirit, fearlessness and zest
for life drive me every day. You are, and will always be, my pride
and my greatest strength.

To my mother,

my inspiration.
You are the wind beneath my wings
and the reason I am able to tell my tales …

AUTHOR'S NOTE

THE YEAR, DATES AND NAMES OF THE OFFICERS-IN-CHARGE and their families have been kept discreet in the book. The aim is to share a life-changing adventure whilst fully respecting the sanctity and privacy of the Indian armed forces and its selfless soldiers.

‘Adventure is worthwhile in itself’

– Amelia Earhart

‘So shut up, live, travel, adventure … and don’t be sorry’

– Jack Kerouac

PREFACE

IN 2019, AN INDIAN AIRFORCE AN-32 AIRCRAFT, WITH thirteen armed forces personnel on board, disappeared over the mountain ranges of Arunachal Pradesh near the Indo–China border. They undertook an extensive mission by air and on foot to trace the aircraft but the thick cloud cover, rapid changes in weather, rugged terrain, deep gorges and valleys along with sparse human habitation and road networks hampered the search-and-rescue efforts. It finally took eight days and 200 sorties for the IAF to spot the wreckage.

Set against this very terrain is the story of six children who went missing in the jungles of Arunachal Pradesh many moons ago, without any gear, food or telecommunication devices. The oldest was thirteen, the youngest six – four girls and two boys.

I was the oldest child in this story.

At the time, we were vacationing in Tawang, a remote military base near the Indo–China border. A picnic had been planned on the day of the events. While that picnic fell through, what unfolded on that day was as nerve-wracking as it was thrilling, and not in any pleasant way.

I've held on to those memories for the longest time, never letting them go because it takes a while – sometimes years – to truly understand how a childhood adventure can impact you.

When I look back, I marvel at how surreal that day had been. It was the kind of misadventure one had only seen in the movies and in all those stories the protagonists were adults, some of whom did not make it. But we were just children, and this was happening to us. And this was as real as it could get.

For years after, numerous existential questions raced through my head: Was God testing us? Were we handpicked for it? Was it preordained? Then the fog started to lift and I saw it for what it was: a day in the jungle. Also, a day when everything went wrong. I'd read somewhere that adversity does not build character, it reveals it. We were tested and pushed to the limits of our physical and emotional endurance. We made it out alive, and it is important that this experience be shared.

Over the years, I have wondered if it was dumb luck or our grit coupled with sheer ingenuity that saved us that day. The terrain was unforgiving, but it let us live. Yes, that is how dangerous those jungles were. And it wasn't just about physical survival. We were at the Indo–China border. We were lost and, for the first five hours, no one knew we were missing. Those five hours were the most crucial. At noon, the cloud cover would become impenetrable and any hopes of being rescued would be dashed. And we certainly would not have survived the night. This was a race against time.

While we did eventually beat the odds and find our way out, the Jungle changed me irrevocably. I made a lot of bad choices that day and all of us were punished because of it. I look back and often call it 'tough love', but only because we didn't die that day.

I was the oldest; the onus of getting everyone out weighed heavily on me. An albatross around my neck, so to speak! It was a lot of pressure for a thirteen-year-old and the dangers were all too real. Truth was, I had consciously led everyone on, and we came very close to dying. Not once, but twice. The Jungle revealed who I was, and it still defines me.

Intrinsically, this is a man-versus-nature or more precisely, a 'teen-versus-nature' survival story, which carries within itself a whole host of life lessons, transformations and epiphanies – physical, psychological and emotional. Told with a touch of humour because, over the years, I have learnt to laugh at myself and not take things too seriously. Years later, when I wrote a novel on boxing which chronicled the protagonist's battle with his childhood demons, I returned to this very memory and tapped into what it had revealed to me.

The Jungle taught me my greatest lessons. Lessons that didn't seem to matter back then but do today. This book is about sharing those lessons whilst taking the readers into the stunningly beautiful yet treacherous terrain of Tawang.

The Jungle was relentless and time was a ticking bomb. Those were the stakes; this is our story. A story that has refused to let go of me. And if I could relive that day, I wouldn't change a single thing. Well, perhaps, I would hold on to the can of Milkmaid a tad tighter …

1

WE THOUGHT WE WERE TRAINED TO SURVIVE THE JUNGLE, except the Jungle hadn't found us yet.

The Jungle was alive. A throbbing entity with its own rules of engagement. And the rules were fairly simple. That you did not try to engage with it and had to let it own you. The Jungle had eyes and ears. It found your fears faster than you found your strength. And word travelled fast. Really fast. Especially if raging waters criss-crossed through its heart. If you did not square off with your fears, the Jungle would square off with you.

But nothing, almost nothing can prepare you for a jungle that doesn't welcome you. I discovered that pretty early, and on a Sunday of all days.

At the time, I was thirteen. Fearless, reckless and raring to take on the world. I believed I could beat all odds and come out on top. One could blame my gender-neutral upbringing or Stan Lee's comics or perhaps both. I was the superhero of my life. I was invincible. Till that Sunday arrived. A day etched so deep in my memory I can summon it at will, teleporting into the heart of Tawang's jungle by simply shutting my eyes.

Tawang was unique in so many ways, as was its jungle – you could not hold your own there. You could not trust it to hold you, either. Literally. They called it 'false vegetation'. It could be discovered only if someone had the misfortune of skidding off the treacherous roads and into the many bottomless valleys, hurtling through layers of clouds. Nothing would break that fall. Not shrubs, not rocks, not even trees. I suppose the Jungle did not allow anyone to intrude and get away with it. Trespassing had consequences. Rocks moved, shrubs were uprooted and trees bent like willows. I know this because nobody I knew had lived to tell the tale. And many a Northeasterner had borne witness to the plummeting ends of both man and his machines. Worse, quite often, the recovery of whatever remained of the dead could not be attempted. The Jungle didn't allow that either.

This is a true account of the day I brazenly led five other children into that Jungle. My thirteen-year-old self simply did not know better, and maybe fortune favours the brave and foolish sometimes. And sometimes … just sometimes, the Jungle that is designed to kill you decides to make you instead.

2

IT WAS MY THIRD VISIT TO TAWANG, HOME TO A TINY military base in Arunachal Pradesh.

The idyllic base was our home every summer, the only time in the entire year when we got to meet our father. A home away from home. A mystical, fantastical land with surreal weather conditions. The roads, if you could call them that, were narrower than a tick's ass and precariously wound around an undulating row of mountains that looked like inverted ice-cream cones, topped with London Dairy's vanilla ice cream. These stoic giants pierced through a sea of translucent cotton-candy clouds and, at 10,000 feet above sea level, Tawang might as well have been the land of fairies and elves where mythical beings and soldiers peacefully co-existed. It certainly was picture perfect, despite the daunting journey that led to it.

To my thirteen-year-old self, getting to Tawang seemed like Harry Potter's journey to Hogwarts, liberally peppered with some edge-of-the-seat thrill of *Mad Max: Fury Road*. It started with a bumpy air-pocket-ridden flight to Guwahati that gave me giant knots in the stomach, followed by a two-day road trip that traversed Tezpur in Assam, ran through the picturesque Tenga Valley, crossing Bomdila Pass at 9,000 feet, slowly climbing up to the literally breathtaking Se-la Pass at 13,000 feet and finally descending into Tawang – meaning the land of the chosen horse.

Fortunately, the forty-eight-hour road journey ensured gradual acclimatization to the decreasing levels of oxygen in the atmosphere. The journey had to be halted at twelve noon sharp as thick, impregnable clouds swooped into the valleys and passes alike, impairing visibility enough to cause fatal accidents. These clouds might have looked innocuous, but they were nasty fellows. Treacherous, vile, whimsical and cruel. They enjoyed playing truant and this whole man-versus-them was a one-way stick-up. Like an old western movie, except, only one of the participants was sanctioned a pistol and if the hapless 'other' so much as moved an inch, the one with the gun drew back quickly. Death was imminent. At these perilous heights, we were the 'others' and these nasty fellows controlled the passes and valleys.

So, noon was the cut-off time for all military movement in the region, unless it were a life-and-death situation, or a war broke out. Most travellers halted at whichever military base they had reached by noon or even drove back a few miles to set camp in one. The journey was resumed the next morning around sunrise, or at 0500 hours, whichever came earlier.

The road to Tawang thrust your phobias right into your face. On my first trip to Tawang, I recall getting off my seat and squatting on the floor of the jeep while crossing Bomdila Pass, just to avoid looking out the window. It was hard to watch the tyres of the moving jeep a few inches away from the bottomless valley without imagining a fall and going up in a gigantic ball of fire.

I suppose the precise moment when death swoops in to snatch your soul isn't actually terrifying. The nanoseconds preceding it are like *Final Destination 6* playing out at 120 frames per second. The jeep hurtling down, with me inside it, being tossed around violently, screaming and watching the free fall knowing that the gas tank has 60 gallons of petrol in it and seeing a protruding rock fifty metres ahead. Now, that is cruel! In the middle of all the screaming, I would also deeply regret not having left a will behind. Yes, even at thirteen, I was the owner of many treasures. A Somerset Maugham and P. G. Wodehouse collection, William Wordsworth and Ruskin Bond, among many other classics, a mini synthesizer, a diary I hoped no adult would ever get their hands on, my rollerblades and a rusty knuckleduster passed down by an older brat. If there had been time, I would bequeath them to my younger sister who, in all likelihood, would trash the knuckleduster and keep the rest. Sudden ends meant no planning and the very idea of being unplanned drove me crazy. I had always hoped to die in my sleep with a peaceful look and a rose-tinted lip balm on, so the idea of having my mangled charred parts picked from a hundred-metre radius was mortifying. That was no way to go if the gods loved you, I reasoned. At thirteen, most of us believed that we were loved. I did go home and write up that will, just in case they didn't.

Anyway, the intrepid Army drivers negotiating this terrain were well versed with the challenges of cruising around turns whilst handling oncoming traffic. The roads were barely two metres wide, and the higher we climbed, the narrower they got. It took some courage and two summers in Tawang to rid myself of the fear of heights. And of course, it didn't help that 'God is Near' was hand-painted in bold yellow lettering on many a mountain bend. One often crossed stone epitaphs erected in the memory of Army men who had lost their lives while traversing these heights. But we were tough Army kids, or so we believed! Army kids or Army brats to the outside world. Irreverent, sometimes more reckless than courageous and unabashedly basking in the reflected glory and adoration that our parents deservedly received. But mostly we were gypsies – agile, quick-witted and a tough bunch of youngsters growing up in a world that barricaded the rest of the universe out and kept us cocooned within ours.

That world was called the cantonment. A heavily guarded, sanitized, self-sufficient neighbourhood created and controlled by the armed forces. Where education meant equal impetus to academics, outdoor sports and co-curricular activities. Cantonments were well-planned mini-townships with zero honking, no traffic snarls, mad markets or hooliganism. They were quiet, clean, orderly havens that might not boast of the Louis Vuitton and Gucci lifestyles that affluent 'civilians' could afford but gave the brats a fuller life experience early in life. The brats moved every two years across the country, from one cantonment to another, inadvertently learning to adapt and engage faster than their 'civilian' counterparts changed their iPhones.

Our wings were our roots.

And those wings had brought my father to Tawang. Being a sensitive base near the border with China, with temperatures dropping to sub-zero during the winters, the officers' families were only allowed to visit during the summer. So Tawang became our home for three summers. Three spectacular summers, new friendships and an accidental adventure that is still fresh in my mind.

Tawang was and is special in so many ways. Ten thousand feet above sea level, home to the oldest monastery in Asia, with clouds that floated right into the military barracks. We were literally living in the clouds. I remembered watching *Jack and the Beanstalk* and was as enthralled as Jack by the first sight of land above the clouds. Tawang to me was just that. Far above and beyond the madding crowds.

The sun rose at 0400 hours and set early too, playing hide and seek all day, often letting the nasty clouds get the better of it. On any given day, one would experience all four seasons, in quick succession. It was fascinating and occasionally frustrating. Given the eccentric weather and sudden rains, the only way to survive at these heights was to set the ground rules and follow them diligently.

The journey back to civilization was often a whole lot faster and just as dramatic. On an MI-17 helicopter and no less! Sitting on top of and around military cargo. The best way to describe the Tawang sojourn was to compare it to a VR game, where one went from *Jack and the Beanstalk* to the land of *Black Hawk Down,* all within nine weeks.

A small part of me hoped the Chinese would spot the chopper, dispatch an anti-aircraft missile to take us. The MI-17 would then go into a tailspin and crash land in Chinese territory. All of us survived it, naturally! My fellow brats and I would go on to make an audacious and fearless attempt at finding our way back home whilst taking down at least a hundred Chinese soldiers. *For what they did at the Galwan Valley recently, they certainly deserved it.*

Alas! No such thing happened. So much for brats romanticizing war movies.

Anyway, the MI-17 made for one hell of a ride. It was a monstrous chopper, more like an armoured tank in the sky. The insides had a few metal seats on either side. Following a first-come-first-served basis, you sat wherever you wanted to. The mothers took the seats and the brats sat on the cold metal floor, among camouflage-green nets, wooden boxes and miscellaneous military cargo. Years later, when my civilian friends in college talked about the adventures they were hoping to have, I would quip cheekily, 'Been there, done that.'

But in that moment, when the large blades started to spin, my heart began to pound furiously and a lump rose in my throat. As the chopper rose, I peered at my father waving from the small helipad made by plateauing a mountain top with the Army's engineering expertise. Some moments stay with you forever. This particular one has stood the test of time.

As we flew off to the safest military base, I stuck my nose against the tiny window and kept waving back till my father became an olive-hued speck on the concrete helipad. Saying goodbye to him was hard. It would be a whole year before I'd see him again. It also didn't help that the military chopper was unpressurized and made my ears pop shut every time. But after all, it was meant to airlift tough soldiers and cargo, not little brats like us who had gotten stranded because flash floods had taken the roads with them and aerial evacuation was the only way to get home safely.

With my popped ears, I could only hear the muffled humming of the MI-17's powerful blades, so I focused my attention on what I could see. As the chopper followed its regular flight path towards Tezpur, I saw snow-capped mountain peaks nestling azure water bodies between them. And since the water was just a few metres below us, there was no mistaking it for something else. Water for the gods – some might've said – and while the peaks were covered in snow, the small lakes had dazzling blue water. That sight, the kind which often appears in heavily photoshopped pictures on Instagram these days, was indescribable. Breathtaking would be an absolute understatement.

I had never witnessed anything like that before or after, and from that summer on, I learnt to accept the mystifying miracles of nature and its inherent fury, in equal parts. And by the time the summer ended, I finally understood what a paradox truly meant.

Tawang was surreal in so many ways. In fact, if it weren't for the Tawang photo album sitting in my closet with scenic pictures of the terrain, those summers could easily have been a figment of my overzealous imagination. But as luck would have it, there were enough godawful pictures of me that permanently marred the surreal world they were shot in. Suffice to say, I looked like a teenage boy, showing early symptoms of what looked like puberty, sprouting unruly weeds over my lips, and if you were to put a gun to my head today, I would beg you to pull the trigger rather than share the damning evidence of those summers. That teenage moustache was the stuff nightmares were made of. So much for my gender-neutral upbringing, Mom and Dad!

Now, straight to that fateful Sunday in June during my last summer in Tawang.

3

WHAT ARE TEENAGE YEARS WITHOUT A TRUCKLOAD OF dramatic realizations: *Dear Lord, what was I thinking*? Or *Mom! Dad! What were you thinking*? Nevertheless, I shall commence with my first recollection of that day and attempt to reconstruct the rest without the inexorable pull of tangential memories, unless they are wildly entertaining, contextual or embarrassing.

Sunday.

The six of us were singing as the one-tonne army truck left the military base. It was a song we had learnt at the adventure camp some weeks ago that brought back memories of the camp for us. I do remember the feeling. Excited, awake, exhilarated and, most of all, happy. Happy to be in the most beautiful place on earth. We believed it unequivocally. I still do.

The sun had just come up across the high peaks. It was 5 a.m. The summer air was crisp like it always was in Tawang and we were wearing our hoodies to beat the chill.

Tawang: The northeasternmost frontier of India, or so we believed, and a stone's throw from Chinese military bunkers. From the Bofors and bunkers on this side, we could wave to the Chinese soldiers on the other side of the border, and we did during a visit organized for us during the camp. And the Chinese always waved back, demolishing my action-driven fantasies about a bunch of brats bringing down a hundred hostile Chinese. *Hundred confirmed kills* on my epitaph! Wasn't happening anytime soon, I rued.

Despite this backdrop, we were hoping to have a rollicking time at the large red bridge along the river. The scarlet colour of the looming metal structure visually broke the undulating green vistas around it. It bridged the gap between two stately mountains that were once a single entity till raging waters split them right down the middle. While the annual flash floods were a couple of weeks away at this point, the banks were wide and safe enough to picnic alongside it. As our real-life action adventure unfolded, it would become apparent that the bridge, the never-ending mountains and water would play both the protagonist and antagonist in the teen versus nature tale that was to follow.

Interestingly, the six of us had recently completed a gruelling two-week adventure camp organized by the Indian Army for the brats whose fathers were posted in Tawang. It was an ingenious way to keep us busy during the summer break and to also toughen us. *Make men out of boys and girls*, they told us.

The day began at 0400 hours and ended sixteen hours later, at 2000 hours. We were trained in martial arts, rifle firing, with old ammunition, of course, horse riding, building a campfire and cooking dal and rice in the wild, all under close supervision. The highlight of the two weeks was seventy-five-odd brats trekking a few miles and finally setting overnight camp right outside the Tawang Monastery. It was a short trek but at the time it had felt like conquering Mount Kilimanjaro.

One cannot talk about treks without mentioning the struggle of bathroom breaks. Especially, if you were the girl with the moochh! *To the outside world, you looked like one of the boys (with little man-boobs) except you weren't. You had to find a rock or a bush to squat behind, praying fervently that a passing scorpion, spider or leech didn't take a fancy to your exposed posterior. Freaking unfair.*

So, after two adrenaline-filled weeks at the camp, we had returned to the barracks, to a feeling of nothingness. The adventure drug had started to wear off and the withdrawal symptoms were excruciating. Painfully long and listless days followed. We needed another 'hit' and I think the Jungle heard us. Loud and clear.

And here we were, the six of us gearing up for a fun-filled Sunday.

Me. *Nidhi with an e*. Fearless, reckless, superhero-ish, had just entered the terrible teens. Suffering from the foot-in-the-mouth disease. Five feet three inches and still growing, or so I hoped. Tina, my nickname for the longest time.

Then there was Mike. Twelve, pragmatic, practical, strong, five feet seven inches tall, still growing, and had a crush on me as I did on him. Ah, well, that was then.

Rohit came next. Twelve again, reed-thin, tall and rarely spoke. Liked to hang around all of us. Hated being photographed. He owned the oddest deadpan expression I had ever come across. A mathematics prodigy.

Next came my younger sister, Neha. Ten, quiet, four feet eleven, praying like hell that she would keep growing vertically. Mercifully, she did! Believed I was invincible. As the day progressed, that notion changed radically … probably. It is another matter that she does not agree and has only a sketchy memory of the day … self-effacing, down to earth, always kind. Fortuitously, that hasn't changed.

Sisters: Mona, eleven, and Gigi, six. I remember them the most.

Mona was the tallest among us. Five feet eight and growing. It was a marvel how someone got that tall that quick! She was timid by disposition, but her height made up for any flaws she might have had. Nobody that tall could be timid, I had reasoned. Well … Mona was a gentle girl.

And Gigi, the pig-tailed baby of the group. Four feet five. Fragile, adorable, with a voice that could melt the most hardened of hearts. Suffice it to say that if I'm able to tell this tale, literally and metaphorically, it is because of little Gigi.

And in this adventurous tale, height did matter.

4

OUR RIDE HAD ARRIVED AT THE OFFICERS' BARRACKS AT exactly forty-five minutes past 0400 hours. We had woken up, showered, packed our food and I was waiting by the window in my father's room-set when the vehicle pulled up, flooding the room with its blinding headlights. Bifurcated into two parts by a large piece of wafer-thin plywood, the room looked like a railway compartment. The part in the front was a miniature living space with a small breakfast table set right in front of a large rectangular glass window overlooking Tawang's breathtaking skyline. During the summer, the table had to be removed and a bunk bed had been added for Neha and me.

As the headlights hit the glass, I shook Neha awake. She had crawled right back into bed, wanting to sleep just a little more. We could not be late for a picnic of all things, I whispered, not wanting to wake up my parents who were sleeping inside.

Having planned and prepared a couple of days in advance and right down to what we'd be wearing, I was ready to go, but before stepping out I opened my diary one last time. Just to see if everything checked out against the list I had made a week ago. I now realize that I developed my habit of planning, down to the very last detail, even for the unexpected and logic-defying contingencies, early on.

Speaking of contingencies, I had once spent an entire week planning and timing a speedy escape from my multi-storey home. In case the ground shook and the earth parted, I'd be ready for it. Yes, I was preparing for an earthquake and the plan seemed simple. With a stopwatch in action, I had pick up my German spitz and make a dash down the staircase and out the door. I had also timed how long it would take to scale the garden wall, whilst holding onto my hapless pooch, who probably thought I had lost my mind, and, importantly, with an emergency-supplies backpack strapped on.

I am surprised word never got out about the sheer ingenuity of my survival games. 'Twas a real shame that India's disaster management units hadn't got wind of my genius yet, I told my terribly amused, and might I add, rather indulgent parents. *I can run that place better than any adult*, I said, with the sometimes-annoying smugness you could only liken to Lucifer from the popular TV series. His pomposity was backed by superhuman powers – I couldn't say the same for me.

Might I additionally emphasize that I had also made contingency plans in the event of a biological war with toxic gases et cetera. Clearly, I had a wildly vivid imagination with a razor-sharp focus on making it out alive. I often pictured myself bursting out of a post-apocalyptic world, in slow motion, with my pooch tucked safely in a backpack. *I Am Legend* being case in point. After all, what was a small human without her pooch? For a girl who craved adventure, the imaginary *Jumanji* bubble was the perfect place to live in. It was my version of the thrilling *Jurassic Park*.

During the lockdown phase, when the COVID-19 contagion brought the world to its knees, I had divided my Mumbai home into two zones. The first one had petty cash, masks, gloves, sanitizers, disinfectant sprays, face shields and a box of toothpicks to press the elevator buttons with contactless elevator idea borrowed from Instagram. I had moved the washing machine into the zone one to immediately disinfect clothes worn outside, even if it were for five minutes. I used the staircase instead of the elevators most of the times. That insidious virus wasn't getting into my home! No, sir! And that is how I kept zone two virus-free.

Oh, yes. Back to picnic checklist then.

- Olive-green jungle trousers and boots. Check.
- Breakfast and lunch sandwiches packed separately. Check.
- Two canned mango-slice tins packed with a can-opener. Check.
- A flask with tea, for the three 'grown ups' in the group. Check.
- Three packets of Parle-G biscuits to go with the tea. Check.
- Four small bottles of Tang for the younglings. Check.

- A tin of Milkmaid, just in case. Well, there was no reason to pack the tin of condensed milk, except that I loved it. Check.
- Digital camera. Check. A small compass that we had no need for. Check.
- Victorinox hunter knife. Check.
- Also check Mike's list before leaving. His list had a small first aid Ziplock bag, three raincoats, in case it rained, bottles of water and some other miscellaneous items.

The six of us huddled outside the barracks, checking our combined supplies. That's when the first important news of the day arrived. And it wasn't good.

P.S. The camera was not put to any use that day. For that matter, nor were the sandwiches, tea, tang and, worst of all, Milkmaid. The wastage of a Milkmaid tin, which I fiercely believe is God's own nectar, was the biggest travesty of all.

5

SOMETIMES THE UNIVERSE GIVES SIGNS, OR A FORESHADOWING. It warns. Sometimes *forthcoming events cast their shadows beforehand.* Momentously happy ones too. But sometimes those signs are just our hearts wanting something so desperately that we project them. All things said, this whole reading-the-signs business can be tricky as hell.

As luck would have it, I didn't read much into the sign that had arrived in the form of a handwritten note.

Sorry, kids, I won't be able to make it to the picnic today. I ate something last night and have taken ill. I'll make it up to you. Promise.

Love,

Pinkie Auntie

I read the note and looked up at Mike and Rohit, exasperated, aghast, rolling my eyes.

'Of course, this had to happen; have you seen how much she hogs?' I exclaimed, shaming our rosy-cheeked, rotund chaperone. 'Couldn't she have sent word last night? How irresponsible!' I crumpled the note in a huff and flung it to the ground. 'Our chaperone has ditched us,' I announced to the group, letting out a loud sigh.

Mike and Rohit exchanged looks, then turned back to me with nonplussed expressions of 'what should we do now'. By then, Neha, Mona and Gigi were already sitting inside the truck.

My mind was racing. All options needed to be explored.

We could wake up the parents and ask them to organize another chaperone or we could cancel the picnic for that Sunday. But once the parents were involved, our picnic was as good as cancelled anyway. No one would volunteer at such short notice especially on a Sunday and, if we cancelled the picnic straight-off, there was not going to be another one that summer. Our vacation was coming to an end and, in seven days, we would be on that air-pocket-ridden flight heading back to New Delhi.

So, on behalf of the group, I reasoned aloud. 'We have the driver and the co-driver. They are responsible men. They know the way.' My voice became high-pitched as my mind became clearer. 'We have food, water, soft drinks,' I reasoned, 'Whatever do we need a chaperone for? She is unreliable as we now know, and we are fauji kids,' I said, rousing the group like a leader, 'We need NO chaperoning. Let's go. It's her loss she's skipped it!'

Mike looked at me sceptically and started to walk towards the truck. 'We don't need a consensus, Mike. Just a decision, and it's taken. What are you doing?' I quipped impatiently. Mike turned around, 'Going on the picnic, Tina. What do we need a chaperone for?'

I beamed at him and eagerly walked towards the truck, happy for having prevailed upon them. Happy because I had taken a clear and perfectly sound decision. I was also definite about one thing: Nobody was going to ruin our picnic today. Nobody.

And this was the first mistake I made that day ...

6

THE ONE-TONNE TRUCK WITH THE DRIVER, THE '*DANDA-MAN*' and the six of us drove out from the barracks and off the base. To explain who is a danda-man (a man with a stick), perhaps a 'one-tonne' truck needs some explaining too. Simply put, the vehicle was a ten-seater olive-painted mid-sized truck with two metal block benches facing each other, perpendicular to the driver's unit ahead that was separated from the seating compartment in the rear by a couple of large hooks near the wheels and connected on the top by a small window with a sliding glass panel. No frills. The vehicle was covered with an olive-coloured hard tarpaulin.

One-tonnes were from an antiquated fleet of the Army's non-combat vehicles, its design dating back to the Second World War. These rugged vehicles were meant to ferry military cargo, troops and miscellaneous items on and off military bases. To get into the back, you had to pull yourself in using a thick rope hanging from the side.

Often, I tested my fitness levels by evaluating the quantum of effort it took to haul myself in. After getting inside the truck, a rugged two-feet-high metal door was latched onto the side with hooks and chains. The rest of the truck was open and, once you sat inside, its rectangular open back framed the outside world like the camera viewfinder in panoramic mode. In my mind, it had an interesting semi-aerial sort of view. These slow fuel guzzlers were regularly pressed into service for a variety of duties, including ferrying the brats to and from army schools.

Since a lot of the army drivers learnt how to drive while on the job, they often drove with a certain devil-may-care-attitude, and so, a danda-man was required to sit in the back.

I still can't figure out the origins of his epithet since he never carried a danda on him. I suppose his job was to supervise and ensure the brats didn't fly out of the vehicle when the driver negotiated blind turns and speed breakers at high speeds.

Sitting beside the half-open gate was a privilege awarded to the tall and strong brats, usually boys over fifteen years of age. I was hoping to earn that seat in another two years, when I got taller. Alas, that didn't happen. Getting taller, I mean.

As the truck turned around a corner, I couldn't help but notice how spectacular the morning was. The sky was clear and showing off its scintillating blueness. Preening, perhaps. The only other time I have seen such colours was years later, while studying in New York. So, there we were, hurtling at a high speed towards our picnic spot. I was sandwiched between Neha and Mike. Happy, wistful but mostly happy. For two reasons: One, the picnic was going to be memorable. It was our last summer in Tawang before my father was posted somewhere else. I wanted to a final breathtaking memory before bidding my goodbyes to the mystical land. We were not coming back anytime soon and I desperately wanted to carry a piece of Tawang back with me, inside one of those magical rectangular musical boxes which, once opened, transported its bearer to the world held inside. Or a snow globe, with Tawang ensconced in the wafting clouds.

Two, my first romance was blossoming that summer – between Mike and me. He was reticent, pragmatic and introverted, while I was impulsive and outspoken, always willing to try something new. Everything was a challenge for me, and I viewed adventures as a stepping stone towards adulthood and was hoping to experience many with him.

Mike and I had also discovered that we were studying at the same Army school and while he knew of me, I had not seen him before. 'Pretty girls rarely pay attention to boys like me,' he said matter-of-factly. 'That's not true,' I protested, blushing at the compliment, aware that he was probably right but for entirely different reasons. I was too wrapped up in playing basketball with my friends, who, by the way, were all boys, to notice, let alone believe that I had any secret admirers. Boys were my buddies, so the butterflies-in-the-stomach affair was alien to me. Alien but welcome. Mike was being self-effacing with his remark about the 'boys like me'. I was drawn to his quiet demeanour and mountain-boy looks. A tiny pug nose and deepset black eyes. I still remember them clearly. He was tall too. A lot taller than me and athletic.

My reverie was interrupted when the truck hit a speedbreaker and we flew off and out of our seats, much like flimsy sunmica furniture during an earthquake. Gigi and Neha fell on the floor of the vehicle and tee-heed together. Mike instinctively grabbed my hand to break my fall. He was strong! My heart skipped a happy beat. I also hoped the danda-man hadn't noticed it. Thankfully, he was busy screaming at the driver. *'Dheere, Ram Niwas. Peeche baccha log hai, tumhara holder nahin!'* He shot angrily in accented Hindi. (There are children in the back, not your luggage!) I pulled my hand away from Mike's before the agitated danda-man turned. That was also when I noticed a dreamy grin on Mike's face. The gods had bestowed the perfect moment to save his summer love. Mike made me happy.

As the truck negotiated another bend, a gust of cold morning air hit our faces. Cool, clean, pure. I would often fill my lungs with it and hold it in as long as I could. Years later, when I saw a major movie star breathing oxygen from a portable cylinder on an international action series set in Mumbai, I was reminded of the lungsful of unadulterated oxygen I had greedily inhaled in Tawang, for free!

We had exited the base and were now descending alongside what would become a river a few kilometres down. I was inside my magical snow globe, witnessing the wonders of nature unfolding in front of my eyes.

I was in love with Tawang. I still am.

I've clung on to every bit of its wonder within the snow globe of my memories, whilst an instrumental music plays in the background. It was a CD that my father played often in his room at the barracks. I had read somewhere that every memory has a soundtrack of its own. 'Tis true! That piece of instrumental music and Tawang are inextricably entwined in my head. I was a mountain girl back then, until I discovered bikinis and beaches in my late teens. Now, I'm a bit of both but mountains will always be my first love.

I smiled while looking at the spectacular vistas and just as we drove around another blind turn, little Gigi started to sing 'Badluram'.

'*Ek khubsurat ladki thi … Usko dekh ke rifleman … Chindi khichna bhul gaya … Havaldar Major dekh liya … Usko pittu lagaya … Badluram ek sipahi thaa.*' The danda-man's eyes lit up; a smile spread across his face as he looked at little Gigi spouting the complicated lyrics. It was the danda-man's regimental song. Gigi's voice had a baby-like quality and, as she got to the chorus, Mike and Rohit started to clap rhythmically and joined in: '*Badluram ka badan zameen ka neeche hai, Badluram ka badan zameen ka neeche hail, toh humey uska ration milta hai.*' As the tempo increased, our danda-man began clapping too.

We'd heard this iconic military marching song of the Assam regiment at the Army adventure camp the same summer. Rousing, energetic and fun-filled was the best way to describe it. The rest of us joined in, singing loudly and clapping hard. An excitement whirled through the air as our voices grew louder. Our danda-man, Barua bhaiya, joined in too! Unfortunately, we couldn't stand up in the moving truck and stomp our boots to add drums to the spontaneous singing. Gigi's baby voice and Neha's melodious rendition had drowned in the thumping claps and 'throw-your-voice' military style singing, but it didn't matter. We were all singing of Badluram! Driver Ram Nivas sang too, but under his breath.

Ek khubsurat ladki thi
Usko dekh ke rifleman
Chindi khichna bhul gaya
Havaldar Major dekh liya
Usko pittu lagaya
Badluram ek sipahi thaa
Japan war me mar gaya
Quarter Master smart thaa
Usney ration nikala
Badluram ka badan zameen ke nichey hain
Toh humein uska ration milta hain
Sabashh … hallelujah
Toh humein uska ration milta hain …

(There was a beautiful girl, seeing whom the rifleman
Forgot to pull the safety catch on a gun
The havildar Major saw him
Sent him on a punishment run with a sack

Badluram was a soldier, who died in the 'Japan' War (WWII)
But our Quartermaster was 'smart'
He got us rations
Badluram's body is now buried
Yet we continue to eat rations drawn in his name
Bravo! … hallelujah …
Yet we continue to eat rations drawn in his name)

We sang the song in a loop as the truck wound around the mountains taking us to the Red Bridge. 'Badluram' remained forever intertwined with our great adventure that summer.

Legend had it that Badluram, an Indian soldier of the Assam regiment, died during the Second World War but his quartermaster, instead of striking his name off the roster, continued to draw rations in his name. When his platoon was surrounded by the Japanese troops in 1944 and their supplies cut off, this extra ration saw the rest of the men through the siege. Badluram saved the day. Hence the lyrics: '*Badluram ka badan zameen ka neeche hai, toh humey uska ration milta hai*'.

Our near-perfect morning was suddenly rocked by the sound of an explosion. We looked at each other with alarm. Was it a landmine? Or an ambush! Having grown up on an army base and devoured war films, my warmongering head hollered with bloodlust. The vehicle trembled and ground to a halt. Ram Nivas, expertly negotiating it to the side of the road, hit the breaks just short of the edge.

As it turned out, the explosion didn't have an action-packed backstory. The danda-man got off and went to investigate as well. The vehicle's bonnet was spewing thick white smoke. It was a sign! Another one, but of course I didn't pay heed.

I got up and looked down at the picturesque valley. We were parked at the edge of the road, overlooking a babbling stream innocuously flowing six to eight feet below road level.

Mike, Rohit and I got off to ask the driver how long it'd take for the vehicle to be fixed. It was nearly 0600 hours. The sun had flooded the valley with golden light that danced playfully on the water below.

As we sat there waiting, we received another piece of news.

The vehicle could not be fixed as an important component under the bonnet had gone kaput! We would have to wait for another vehicle to come by. The danda-man was going to walk back to base and get another vehicle to pick us up. And just like that, it was a tragic end to a glorious day.

How could this be happening, I muttered angrily. It seemed like we were not meant to go on this picnic at all.

Destiny and all were fine but free will meant something, right?! When the going got tough, the tough got going, right? The inside of my head felt like a war zone, with missiles and bullets flying in from all directions, and I was at the centre of that mayhem, ducking whilst trying to work out a plan of action. *Call of Duty: Warzone,* only in virtual reality. I had to think of a way out, there had to be a way!

Looking thoughtfully at the stream below, my eyes beamed with fresh hope all of a sudden. I turned towards Mike and Rohit, all fired up! This was not how our picnic would end today. Definitely not.

Destiny be damned. I had a plan and it was time to take absolute charge.

P.S. The Jungle had a plan too and from there on, the Jungle was in charge. I just didn't know it yet. Worse still, I was about to commit my second mistake. And the Jungle lay in wait …

7

THE PLAN WAS SIMPLE. DITCH THE ONE-TONNE TRUCK and continue the rest of the journey on foot. Not along the winding roads though. That would take an eternity and more.

I turned to Mike, whose eyes widened with uncertainty but I didn't wait to explain. My mind was made up. Walking up to the driver with renewed vigour, I rattled out the grand plan meant to save the day. Ram Nivas looked at me. There was a studied pause. '*Didi, aap yeh mat karo please*,' he urged me politely not to go ahead. There was an unsettling urgency in his voice.

Taking a deep breath, I looked reflectively towards the horizon, whilst mentally exploring all our options. As far as I could see, there was only one that led to our picnic. I looked at the mountains and the stream below to get some sort of a nod, a sign. Mountains do talk to you. Especially the weathering ones that have held their ground for centuries. The water was flowing languorously, oblivious to the storm brewing in my head. 'We picnic here?' Gigi asked suddenly. And in a flash, it all became crystal clear.

'Hell, no, we don't!' I shot back and turned to the only adult on the scene.

'*Bhaiya, hum yahan se paani ka peecha karte huye Red Bridge tak pahunch jayenge. Aap danda-man bhaiya ka yahin wait karo*,' I said with firm finality, explaining how we were going to follow the stream and get to the Red Bridge and that he should wait near the vehicle until the danda-man arrived with the replacement.

Mike and Rohit walked into the one-sided conversation. The harried driver looked urgently at the two of them. He was understandably worried. His neck would be on the line if anything happened to us, so he earnestly tried to convince me that the replacement vehicle would arrive soon, after which we could carry on with our picnic at the Red Bridge. He was secretly hoping I wouldn't set some crazy plan into motion. The thing was, he was only trying to stall us. By the time the replacement arrived, we would have to head back to base. He knew it, I knew it.

Realizing his conundrum, I added softly, 'Don't worry, *bhaiya, humme kuch nahin hoga, aap doosri one-tonne ko leke Red Bridge pe pohunch jana. Hum aapko wahan milenge*.' I'd politely asked him to simply drive the replacement vehicle to the assigned picnic spot where we'd meet them.

'Picnic time, guys, let's go!' I hollered, while heading back to the others, ignoring Ram Nivas' body language that gave away his frustration. He was clearly at his wit's end with no way to relay a message back either. Did I bully him? Absolutely, but at the time I felt no need to apologize to someone who was getting in the way. In hindsight, I feel bad for having put him in such a difficult position. He was only trying to protect us. *Sorry, Bhaiya!*

'Tie up your boot laces tightly, kiddos, we are going on a little adventure,' I said, with the dogged surety of a general who knew what he was doing. *Ha! General Don Quixote, more like it.*

'What's the plan? What adventure?' Mona asked, in a jittery voice. I let out a deep sigh and looked at her, wondering why she didn't like to take any risks. She was a nice girl, so I answered patiently, 'We follow the stream and reach the Red Bridge.' Mona looked down, trying to make sense of my master plan. I added perkily, 'There is plenty of space to walk alongside. It'll take longer on foot, but we will get there easily and this will be a lot more fun.'

Neha looked down at the stream and quipped, 'Good plan, Didi.' Energized, I turned to Mike and Rohit next, 'Come on, guys, we are in our jungle boots; we have food and water and the plan is simple and easy. We follow the stream and reach our picnic spot. Let's not waste time and ruin our last Sunday in Tawang or,' and I added with a studied pause, 'We could plonk ourselves right here by the road and picnic away. Why do we need to tell anyone that we were too scared to walk along a stream?' I added with mocking finality.

I had everyone's attention now.

And then I rolled in the wrecking ball, 'What kind of Army brats fear a stream in a jungle they know?' *The Jungle silently sniggered.*

'We fear nothing,' Neha said resolutely and bent down to tie her shoelaces. Gigi started to tie hers too. The two were thick! Seeing the little ones in the group raring to go, the rest relented immediately.

'Let's go, guys, we've lost enough time as it is,' I said, visibly charged up, and walked back to the one-tonne to check if I had left anything inside. Mike and Mona did a quick check of our picnic inventory too. We were good to go.

Martin Luther King, Jr had said that a genuine leader was not a searcher for consensus but a moulder of one. I didn't understand these lofty ideas back then, but the facts were thus: I had planned the picnic down to the last detail and I was going to take it to its logical conclusion, determined to take back one final memory of the place I knew I would never visit again. I fed off that kind of nostalgia a lot. What are we if not the summation of memories that get etched on to our faces, showing up as deep lines and scars with the passage of time?

Taking the first step down the treacherous slope like a sure-footed mountain goat, although there were none in the region, I led the others confidently. They believed in my plan and that was enough for me. I would lead from the front and take the brunt of whatever came our way.

So, in keeping with the rule of the animal kingdom, where the young are often placed in the middle of the moving herd for protection, Gigi and Neha walked in the middle as we trudged ahead in a single file – I, Rohit, Gigi, Neha, Mona and, finally, Mike.

It was a mere twenty-foot drop to the stream below. We had attempted over hundred feet at the adventure camp, so this felt like a cakewalk in comparison. Or so it seemed.

And thus, began our descent into hell. Ram Nivas, our harried driver, watched us disappear down the mountain. Perhaps concern and disgruntlement welled up inside him, but he didn't say. Truth be told, even he couldn't have guessed what awaited us that day.

The Jungle was smiling viciously.

P.S. I've often wondered that if I could go back in time, would I make the same decisions? I think I would. After all, we all make bad decisions and some of them snowball into cataclysms far bigger than we could have imagined and beyond our control. We still make them because they are meant to be made; they are meant to reveal who we are …

8

Four weeks ago.
Army Adventure Camp, Tawang

AN ESSENTIAL DETOUR.

Tangentially, or maybe not quite, back at the Army adventure camp, we were imparted firing lessons. How could *fauji* kids not know how to handle a weapon and hence … we lay prostrate on the ground, eight to a row, bellies down, gripping the heavy rifle tightly, its butt plate wedged deep and hard into our right shoulders and aimed at the black target sheet cutouts shaped in the likeness of the enemy's torso. These faceless cardboard cutouts were attached to little sticks at the far end, where the undulating earth rose into a hillock. Three magazines were allotted per 'cadet'.

We all pressed the trigger together when the *ustaad* screamed 'fire'. There was a hard recoil as the hot bullet shells fell out. My performance was nothing short of downright pathetic. A shame since my father, by all accounts, belonged in a Clint Eastwood western. Firing from the hip, bullseye each time. His awestruck colleagues and juniors spoke of his skills on the firing range. Even my mother had won a medal for marksmanship back in school. And here I was. A big zero in firing!

Now I was the top of my class in karate, rock climbing, horse riding, athletics and had my eyes set on the Young Lion Excellence Cup at the end of camp. And today's epic debacle at the shooting range was going to come in the way. Mike had all bullseyes. I squinted my eyes to spot where the bullets I fired had disappeared. Into thin air, perhaps, and nowhere near the targetsheet. My pride was hurt.

In my defence, being 'southpaw,' I had been struggling with the butt plate on my right shoulder and turned around to the Junior Commissioned Officer (JCO) standing behind me, '*Sahab*, I cannot use my right hand as well as my left, could you please find someone who can tell me how to use the rifle left-handed?' I looked on, as the two JCO's in charge, neither of whom had ever trained anyone left-handed, quietly discussed how they would help me. 'But this rifle, it is not meant to…' one said under his breath. They stepped away, conferring privately as one of them moved the rifle to my left shoulder. 'Fire!' He hollered. And, I did. After my left shoulder had taken the full impact of the rifle's recoil, I set it down and looked up triumphantly at the targetsheet. 'Did you see, sir?' I exclaimed, breathless with excitement while the JCO behind me was attempting to see if I had really hit bullseye. In a weird rush of teenage hormones, I then jumped up and, in a flash, started running towards my target sheet.

'Hold fire, hold fire!' the panic-stricken JCOs screamed in unison and blew their whistles hard. A few kids were still shooting and disaster was ready to unfold. For the men training us, everything was moving in slow-motion, phantom-cam style, 300 frames per minute of pure shock. Something hit the targetsheet, a mere seven-odd feet away from mine. It was a bullet from someone's rifle who had not heard the 'hold fire' soon enough.

To this day, I do not remember hearing 'hold fire' either. I ran those hundred-odd feet towards the edge of the hillock in a daze. I didn't hear the panic-stricken cries of Neha from the sidelines either.

The firing had stopped and the JCOs were gobsmacked by what had just unfolded. Nonplussed, I ran back to them with my target cardboard, the mark of the bullet on it, 'I told you, sir, left is my strong arm.'

One of the JCOs shot back, '*Goli lag sakti thi* (you could have been hit),' to which I had cheekily quipped, 'it is expired … ammunition *Sahab* … err … sir.' The indignant JCO shook his head and called out for the captain in charge of the camp. '*Jai Hind*, Sir,' they said in unison as the captain arrived. Their heads would have been on the line had I taken a bullet. The captain's too.

There was hushed silence all around. Neha looked at me, making it visibly clear she did not approve of my recklessness. I heard someone among the group of kids whisper 'crazy'. I didn't care. I was feeling exhilarated.

In hindsight, I wasn't thinking about the danger I had put myself into and the gross disregard for my own safety. I was impetuously focused on explaining exactly why I should be taught left-handed. So that I could ace in shooting too. I remember rambling about this when I was hauled up by the irate captain. I even recall Mike giving me a dismissive look as I cockily whispered later, 'I knew I wasn't going to get hit.' *Like hell!*

The captain gave me the dressing down of my life, 'If you were an officer in my battalion, Sharma, I would put you in the Quarter Guard for a week,' he yelled in the quintessential army baritone. I was holding up the target sheet feebly attempting to explain my actions, to which he had seethed in a steely cold voice, 'I'd rather have an average soldier who takes orders, than a brilliant one who's rogue. What you have done is dangerous, Sharma. Trigger happy. Off the ground, NOW!'

What happened next, how word of my brazen recklessness travelled home and how I was suitably punished is a tale for another time. But history was about to repeat itself, and prophetically so. This time around, I was leading five little people into a jungle I knew nothing about, all in the quest for that perfect picnic.

The jungle was Darth Vader and in the real world, Darth Vaders never lost. And definitely not to an arrogant and reckless thirteen-year-old who had learnt nothing from a firing debacle …

9

WE REACHED THE STREAM BELOW AND LOOKED AT WHAT lay ahead.

'Are you excited, Gigi?' I asked, to which the little munchkin nodded, her cherubic smile lighting up her face and mine too. She turned to Mona, 'Tang, didi.' I looked on as she glugged her favourite drink straight from the plastic bottle. It was satisfying to watch her and Neha relish the tangy refreshment. In hindsight, I am relieved they had their fill.

We had reached the bottom of the mountain and the way ahead was clear. There was a long-enough stretch of the pebbled path that would take us to the Red Bridge without a hitch. I looked across the stream at the Jungle: green, thick, alive.

Trees talk if you care to listen. I know that now but back then, I had only heard the old oak tree outside my window back home. I'd heard it breathe. Yes, breathe. On the cold nights when I sat up prepping for my exams, when the rest of the world fell into a deep slumber, I heard the Old Oak: like an old man, a bit eerily, breathing, laboured and arrhythmic. I wasn't hallucinating; I picked up my stopwatch to check for a pattern and there was one. A clear and loud inhalation and exhalation, almost human-like. I wondered if the Old Oak was trying to communicate with me. Tell me its story? Perhaps, some secrets about the things it had seen. Had it suffered? But trees inside cantonments flourished. They were looked after.

'Ready, everyone?' I quipped excitedly and started walking along the stream. It was nearly 0700 hours on my watch, we were running late by an hour, but it wasn't the thing we needed to worry about. For the moment, time was on our side.

The pebbles under our feet constantly moved as we started to follow the stream towards the Red Bridge. I could hear the jungle birds sing their joyous songs from the other side of the stream. *What did they sing about*, I wondered and smiled at little Gigi and Neha, hoping they were enjoying it as much as me. The two were chirping away about their barbie doll collection. Being older, Neha had amassed many more and promised Gigi to send her some once she got home. I smiled and turned my attention back to our surroundings. What a spectacular morning it was! We were incredibly fortunate to be breathing and living this moment fully. A moment that would never come again.

It was going to be a long walk along the stream, with many twists and turns, some expected ones, some straight out of *Fear Factor*. The universe was going to do everything in its power to rein me in. To teach me that I wasn't above the rules of the Jungle. To tame me. To get me to 'bend the knee' if you will.

But should I have? And did I?

P.S. The knee ... But more on that later, a lot more ...

10

THE ONE-TONNE BREAKING DOWN TRIGGERED A SUDDEN turn of events and the new course of action galvanized all of us. A trek, a river walk, a jungle *darshan* and a picnic at the end of it, all rolled into one. This was better than our original, droll plan of driving down to the Red Bridge to spend the entire day by its banks, I thought happily.

A few weeks ago, seventy-five of us had undertaken an all-day trek during the adventure camp, at the end of which, we had pitched our tents overnight, a few metres from the stunning Tawang Monastery. Only that time, we were under the strict supervision of a dozen chaperones. It was to ensure the unruly bunch would not 'trek' themselves into gorges and ravines. This, now, was definitely more fun.

I cannot speak for the five, but my senses came alive as we continued walking. The soothing sound of waters running gently over weathered stones, the rustle of trees as the morning breeze woke them up, the sky so clear and blue as if it had rained the night before, the harmonious bird calls, the kind of pristine beauty that the COVID-triggered lockdown has taught me never to take for granted ever again.

In retrospect, it feels surreal to have lived that day. To have taken the decisions I took. And to have come out alive.

'Look!' Mona pointed urgently at something as we continued walking. I looked across the stream and saw the vegetation rustle. 'We don't have tigers in Tawang,' Rohit said softly. I think he had a crush on the leggy Mona. Just then, a mountain dog popped its scruffy head out. He was looking at the intruders with rapt attention. 'It's like a bear,' Gigi said with a happy spark in her eyes, 'Is it a he-dog or a she-dog, didi?' Her child-like curiosity made us all smile. 'It looks like a he-dog, Gigi, scruffy and large,' I replied confidently. Unlike the grand misadventure I was leading everyone into, this confidence was not misplaced.

Most armed forces families are incomplete without their dogs: lazy labradors, majestic German shepherds, intimidating dobermans, aggressive Lhasa apsos, temperamental German spitzes and robust pye-dogs. And most Army brats grow up around them. An officer's dog will have a litter and suddenly six other army families will enjoy its furry fruits. The army is a dog-loving community.

Growing up, I had three amazing dogs with distinct personalities. One of them was a randy mid-sized German spitz called Snoopy, father to countless puppies within a one-mile radius of our home in the cantonment. No lock could keep Snoopy in, no wall was too high. In the summer months, he slept besides his knell in the garden. His nocturnal rendezvous became the talk of town when he snuck into a fellow officer's garden to sow his wild oats with Debbie the Doberman, who was twice his size. Snoopy was as unapologetic as my mother was embarrassed when the officer's wife came home. She feared for Snoopy's life, she told my mother diplomatically.

The other gem was Tawang's gift to us: A tiny purebred Apso, whom we called Mickey. A beautiful ball of white fur, a hopping rabbit, with heart-melting puppy eyes hidden behind shaggy Apso hair, perfect in all ways, well almost. Except Mickey's farts were so potent and loud, it was hard to believe a pint-sized dog was capable of generating such toxic fumes. Strangely, he saved his best ones for the weekly ladies' get-together at home. 'Your dog is dangerous,' one of the ladies said laughingly to my mother. 'This fellow will break wind and run off and we'll be left wondering which one of us did it.' The modus operandi was simple. He would come hopping into the living room for tasty treats and while the ladies were fawning over him, Mickey broke wind. There was a hushed silence as the fumes spread quickly, and the ladies silently wondered which one of them was the uncouth culprit. It took them a few visits to figure this out, by which time Mickey the Fartonator had been confined to the veranda.

My poor mother was always at the receiving end courtesy our dogs and, well, me!

'How do you know it's a he-dog, Tina didi?' Gigi asked. I looked at the dog across and realized he was walking with us on the other side. From a distance, his face was inscrutable. Was he happy to see us or was he following his next meal? Mountain dogs could be vicious too. 'She-dogs look gentler, more like girls, Gigi,' I tried explaining. I wondered how to explain it to a six-year-old, 'Well, they're prettier; they have kind, beautiful eyes, like a deer, or like you, Gigi.' Now that made sense to her as she looked at the dog across the waters, 'He is big and scary, like a bear, and so hairy. I'll call him Bhalu.' We all concurred. Bhalu looked like an unkempt, wild version of the most majestic dog I had ever laid eyes on – her name was Grace.

My Grace. A German shepherd, a monster puppy who grew up to be a lady. Forever remembered fondly (by me) for taking regular puppy-sized dumps in Neha's slippers and shoes, for being the reason Neha and I would have to figure innovative ways to save ourselves and run for cover if she were in the vicinity, for chewing up our toes like her life depended on it, for shredding curtains, socks, shoes and anything she could get a hold of with rare delight, for a bark so fierce yet feminine that people feared pressing the bell at our gates. For also being my mother's shadow all day. Following her, waiting for her in the stairwell and then walking up only when she started to climb. Recently, I chanced upon a Thomas Hardy poem, 'A Popular Personage at Home,' that best described her. 'No doubt I shall always cross this sill/ And turn the corner, and stand steady/ Gazing back for my mistress till/ She reaches where I have already run.' That was the intelligent and incredibly strong Grace who would often hold her own leash in her mouth so neither Neha nor I could catch her, as she ran in circles in the garden.

Grace made up for Randy Snoopy and Mickey the Fartonator. When she passed on at the grand age of fifteen, just after I had returned from the film school in New York, we swore never to keep another dog. Her passing was traumatic. I still have not donated the yellow raincoat I had bought for her in New York. She passed away before the monsoons and unfortunately never got to wear it. Not that she would have fancied one, dogs love the rain.

My reverie was suddenly broken by the neighbour's barking dog and I think back to Bhalu on the other side of the stream that day.

Was Bhalu protecting us? Was he our lucky mascot? Or was he simply being a dog, happy to have found human company. We were going to find out soon.

11

0800 hours

SPLASHING MY FACE WITH COLD MOUNTAIN WATER, I GULPED a few handfuls. The taste of that water is a big part of my memories of Tawang. More refreshing than any bottled water peddled by large corporations. Every tastebud in my mouth celebrated its purity. Loaded with natural minerals and a sweetness I've not tasted since.

It had been an hour since we had started walking, and the hour had passed quickly. Bhalu was tailing us from across the stream and Gigi calling out to him lovingly. His scruffy tail wagging from side to side confirmed their camaraderie. Neha and Mona gossiped about Pinki Auntie, our 'ditcher chaperone' with her fancy leather boots. 'I saw her laughing with that good-looking bachelor uncle that day,' Mona added conspiratorially. Neha and Gigi's eyes widened at the revelation. 'Is he the one who was playing the guitar at the party?' Neha enquired. Mona nodded mischievously. Then the three chuckled together. Pre-teen gossip was so inane.

That summer at the camp, we had gossiped about a spoilt brat who had tried to threaten the captain in charge of the camp, for pulling her up for running late every morning. She had a room to herself while the rest of us bunked together in a dorm! 'I'll have your pips stripped off,' she had told him arrogantly while we looked on aghast! 'No, she did not say that to him,' we whispered wide-eyed. He had laughed in her face and asked her to give it a shot. And all this while, we had thought the young captain and she were an item of sorts! What a disappointment it was for the younglings! We had only wanted to take home juicy tales about a college student, a beautiful one at that, and the young, swashbuckling Army captain who had given me the dressing-down of my life.

'Five-minute break, guys,' I announced while looking at my watch. Mike was doing his own calculation and said, 'We'll make it to the bridge by brunch time I suppose.' I smiled and chirped back, 'Way sooner.' Just then, a large vehicle went past on the road above. From the heavy rattle, it sounded like a three-tonne truck.

'Could that be our replacement vehicle?' I wondered aloud. Mike shook his head from side to side, 'Dandaman would still be walking back to base. It's only been an hour,' to which Mona added, 'unless he hitched a ride from someone heading back to base …' Yes, that could have been possible too. But it wasn't our replacement vehicle, or they could have spotted us.

Gigi and Neha had opened the drawstring bags to eat.

Bhalu sat down at the other end, enthusiastically hoping for a treat too. I wondered if he had been domesticated at some point. 'Bhalu wants to eat,' Gigi said, looking at him and promptly hurled a sandwich across the stream.

Understandably, it didn't reach Bhalu and fell with a plopping sound into the water and got swept away. 'Don't waste food, Gigi,' Mona chided her younger sister. 'But Bhalu must be hungry also,' Gigi protested while wolfing down down on a sandwich and pestering her big sister to feed him. 'Pleaseeee.' The task was easier for the long-legged Mona, who picked up a small stone, pushed it into an open packet of Parle-G biscuits and hurled it across. The packet landed near Bhalu, who sniffed them for a few seconds and then turned his head away. Parle-G didn't quite cut it with the fussy mutt.

Mona looked back at Gigi mock-accusingly. 'Your Bhalu wasted my favourite biscuits and now I am hungry.' Neha shook her head disapprovingly while taking a quick bite.

A dissed Gigi looked on, disappointed, 'But why, he doesn't like it?' she wondered sheepishly. 'Because he is a big bear Gigi, and like bears, Bhalu likes honey so no throwing food, okay?' Their banter made us all smile. It was time to go.

Neha handed me a sandwich, but I wasn't hungry, nor were the boys. We'd eat once we got to the bridge.

'Your laces,' I said, pointing to Mona's jungle boots. They had come undone a third time. 'Cross them and wrap them around the top of the shoe a few times, then tie them tight,' I instructed her, pointing to how I had done mine. My jungle boots acquired at the adventure camp were my prized possession. Light weight, olive-green ones.

As a kid, I was fascinated by the Army boots my father wore and would often step into them. He made the boots look so incredibly cool but when I slipped my tiny feet into them and tried to move around, I would tumble over. They were awfully hard on the inside and heavy but I never stopped trying them on. I was stubborn like a mule, for want of a better idiom. I was thereafter nicknamed the 'boot-chor' (boot-thief) *because his hard-black leather boots would disappear from the shoe rack and be later found in my room every single time.*

I looked at my boots with child-like exuberance. These were my first pair, one that fit me perfectly and I cherished them till the soles gave way a couple of years later. I have never lost my fascination for all things olive-coloured. I would bleed olive-green any day. *Years later, I found a pair my size and started to wear them to college only to develop deep purple bruises around my heels and scars that took over a year to heal. How did soldiers wear them and never look uncomfortable? I still wonder.*

As we began walking again, I shot a look at the steep mountain side and observed that the road we had descended to reach the stream below, seemed much further up than when we'd started walking. 'How high is it?' I asked Mike. Rohit looked up too. 'Maybe eighteen to twenty feet.' The mathematician of the group had spoken. A boy of few words. I trusted his calculation. Word was that he had topped in mathematics for three consecutive years back at the Kendriya Vidyalaya. I somehow equated his expertise in math with the ability to measure the height of a mountain with just his eyes.

It seemed we had descended quite a bit. Even if I were to wade right into the middle of the stream and crane my neck sixty degrees, the road would no longer be visible. However, the rumble of heavy vehicles passing overhead and their mild vibrations we felt down by the stream was enough existence of its existence. The stream still skirted the road above.

As we continued walking, the pebbles by the bank made a pleasant crunching sound under our feet. Their edges were polished to perfection by the continual friction of the water – revealing their innermost colours like polished diamonds.

A particular stone caught my attention. It was shining among a sea of smooth grey ones. Picking it up, I gaped at it. This one was grey in colour like all the others except it had bands of iridescent blue running across its width. The bands were the same magnificent hue of blue as the skies above. Did it break and fall from the skies and soak up the grey from its common companions? Was this some kind of fall from grace, because it really didn't seem to belong where I found it.

I smiled at the treasure I had chanced upon and popped it in the bag on my shoulder. This was going back with me to stay forever.

I learned later that the memories associated with joy,

shame, fear, love or grief get seared into the amygdala of the brain with little to no assistance from technology, namely cameras.

And often the most incredible moments and memories: your first awkward kiss, the time a reef fish in the Koh Samui waters mistook you for food while you were snorkelling and bit you senseless, the euphoric look on your father's face when he got a call from the dean informing him that you had topped the university despite being written off by your teachers in school or the year you spent working on an independent film in Los Angeles whilst sharing an apartment with a half-African-American half-Korean former exotic dancer who was as kind as she was beautiful. These moments never happen when the camera is pointing at you and rolling. And rightly so. These moments and how they impacted you and made you feel, belong to you alone and they remain ensconced and embedded in the deepest recesses of your memories, to be conjured at will.

Isn't it absolutely beautiful that some moments exist only for you and are gone when your time is up? I believe an expiration date ain't a bad thing. It makes the memory ephemeral and also magical. Then, poof!

But sometimes, an event is so powerful and transformative that you are unable to hold it inside of you. It grows in significance as the years go by and it forces its way out because it absolutely must. Or, because you feel the absolute need to chronicle it for posterity. And your 'amygdala-ic' memory doesn't let you down, even if technology does.

That extraordinary stone I picked up from the side of the stream that day was only mine to cherish and remember.

That it never left its idyllic home is an altogether different matter. I suppose, an object of such rare beauty was not meant to sit on a common mantelpiece.

As we continued to walk, I noticed that the mountain on our side had banked a hard right. Rather unusual, I mused. It had seemed like a straight and gradual descent along the stream so far. I reckoned the roads above us were winding around the stately mountain at much faster and consistent intervals.

The journey ahead was about to get hard could best be described as a colossal understatement.

Looking across the stream, I noticed Bhalu was gone. Was he disappointed we'd offered him the humble Parle-G biscuits? Had he gotten bored of following us or had he sensed something amiss? I wondered but said nothing, lest I upset little Gigi.

But as we trudged around the mountain bend, Neha was the first to notice the absence of our furry companion. 'Where is Bhalu?' And thus began the chatter and conspiracy theories about where the mountain creature had vamoosed and why. Neha and Mona's, to be more specific. But I had other things on my mind.

It was a splendid morning and I felt this sudden impulse to fish out the digital camera and capture that transcendent moment in time but didn't. Finding that perfect foreground to the paradisiac background, the most fitting angle and light for the shot and worse still, photobombing the scenic view and desecrating it with my moochh-face. It would've slowed us down, like picture-taking sessions often do. And that's exactly the sort of slacking we didn't need. Specially not in uncharted territory. There would be plenty of time once we reached our picnic spot, I reasoned internally. In hindsight, it wouldn't matter.

Putting thoughts of Bhalu's sudden disappearance aside, I focused on the path ahead. As the 'team leader', it was my job to make a success of the day.

P.S. What I didn't sense was that the Jungle was smirking and about to teach a thirteen-year-old the lesson of her life.

12

SOON AFTER BHALU DROPPED OUT OF SIGHT, THE MOUNTAIN banked a hard right. At the time, there didn't seem to be any plausible connection, but the sudden turn of events didn't seem astonishing or remarkable anymore.

As was typical of Tawang's temperamental weather, it had become windy and I noticed that as the water and air mixed with vigour, the stream had started to bubble up and foam. Grey rocks jutting out aiding further in the frothing. The stream had also widened. Slyly so.

Aristotle said in his *Poetics*, 'surprising yet inevitable' and, while he said this with reference to ideal endings in good pieces of writing, a surprising yet inevitable narrative was unfolding right now, and our journey was far from the end. And certainly not the kind of end we could have imagined.

The stream was no longer a couple of feet wide. Now nearly thrice that width, it had expanded so gradually and surreptitiously that its dilation had escaped our attention entirely.

While I was still mulling over the changes in our immediate terrain, a drop of water fell from the sky and landed on the tip of my nose. Then another, and many others. My face was quickly soaked as the drops coalesced together to run into my eyes and drip down my chin.

13

NEHA LOOKED UP AT THE SKY WITH UNBRIDLED JOY AND spread her palms out to catch the raindrops. Who didn't love the magic of the rains in the mountains and the mist that wafted in as a result! Except we didn't need the rain or mist or clouds right now. What we doubtlessly needed were clear skies, good visibility and an easy descent to the Red Bridge by the river, our predestined picnic spot.

Now, it was a no-brainer that rains brought hope and life for every living being – a unique symbol of the intelligent design of our planet. Without rain, most of the land in the world would be a vast, parched desert. What was also true was that too much of it could ruin the most meticulous of plans. It certainly was threatening ours.

As the showers went from a light drizzle to a mild downpour, we took refuge under a jagged slab-shaped rock protruding from the side of the mountain.

Mike opened his bag promptly and Gigi, Neha and Mona were handed their shiny 'foreign' raincoats purchased by their parents from the markets of Bagdogra. Affordable yet stylish. Neha outgrew her shimmery turquoise-blue waterproof jacket but it's still tucked away in a closet somewhere. Too pretty, too many memories of magical monsoons lingering on its glossy material.

The rain lashed hard for a few minutes but went away as quickly as it had arrived. Relieved, we emerged from our temporary shelter and began walking again. As inevitable as the rain was in this part of the world, for the first time, it did kick up some anxiety. What if it started to rain again and this time it didn't stop? We'd have to turn around and head back the way we came. And what a waste that would be, besides a big embarrassing question mark on my teen judgement. I hoped fervently that it wouldn't rain again.

With the downpour, the pebbles under our feet had become slippery, the stream had swollen up and started bulging at its seams and the walking path had shrunk with the water pulling in chunks of soft mud and flora along with it. I was eyeing the water with admiration and trepidation.

There was nothing more alive than the water. A billion drops confidently winding and flowing through the mountainous jungle, slicing through it defiantly, monsoon after monsoon. A ribbon of pale blue and translucent froth, happily splashing away downstream, blissfully unaware that their happy-go-lucky and independent disposition would become subservient to the oceans, sooner or later.

We were now walking in a row. It was the only way to keep going since the water had gained considerable turf.

There was a loud gush from up ahead and I wondered what lay beyond the approaching mountain bend.

I could never have guessed.

Perhaps, it does take a lifetime of experience to sense what is coming before it does. To anticipate. To have an alternate plan in place. As we walked further, negotiating the hard left turn, I was the first to see it. And I froze.

This was supposed to be a straight path to the Red Bridge. It was supposed to be a nice, memorable walk along the stream. We were supposed to enjoy the warmth of the sun, light filtering through the trees and dancing playfully on the waters. We were supposed to capture the magnificence of nature in all its glory and take back beauteous memories. We were supposed to enjoy our banter and halt occasionally to eat our sweetened sandwiches, drink Tang and saunter on. It was our last summer here. Could it not have been a little uncomplicated and painless?

Mike, Rohit and I looked at each other, clammed up and panicking inside. My thirteen-year-old head was abuzz. This was a curveball straight out of the purgatory. I was indignant looking at what lay ahead.

Our designated walking path, now strip, had been wholly swallowed up by the gushing waters. Not an inch was left to walk on.

Like a python stretching its flexible jaws to swallow a prey many times its size, the water had swallowed up our picnic whole and laid waste to all our plans. This was a dead end.

P.S. This was also an inflection point in my personal journey. Literally and metaphorically. Against better sense or advice, I had led five children, all of them younger than me, on a picnic which was now not meant to be. In hindsight, I had made one mistake after another, which had now brought us all to this particular impasse.

The plan had failed.

In retrospect, I envisage that meticulous planning is imperative and plans ought to be made, but it would be a tad bit foolhardy to expect the powers that be to do your bidding. To dance to our tunes if you will, to not boomerang. Even the most well-intentioned plans have been known to! And, in all likelihood, the only thing we will ever have any real control over is that first definite step we take towards our end game. After that, expect only the unexpected!

The element of chance, random events, enticing distractions and unforeseen upsets. Like locusts, they will swarm in. They will throw us off, derail our plans and remorselessly destroy them. It will entirely be up to us to accede to that derailment, to surrender, to throw in the towel.

However, if we choose to confront, to push back hard, we need to be ready for the proverbial trial by fire. Or water, or mountains (as was the case here).

My trial-by-fire moment had arrived suddenly.

Would I regret what I was about to do next? Did I do the right thing? Would I do it again? Was this my Don Quixote moment? Yes, yes, yes and errr … yes.

14

SCRUTINIZING OUR NOW NON-EXISTENT PATH AHEAD, I noticed a large grey rock jutting out from the mountain, bursting forth from the side, precisely at the point of the sharp left turn. As per Rohit's calculation, it was nearly seven feet from ground level, except there was no ground under it, just water.

Our erstwhile path was a waterway now, the shrubs from the mountain caressing its restless fluidity.

The 'stream', if I could still call it that, had gone from a few feet to nearly thirty feet wide over the past couple of hours. Like the self-configuring autobots from *Transformers*, it had turned into an intimidating adversary, ready to push us back, to take us on, should the need arise. The size wouldn't have mattered if it had not eaten up our path and brought our odyssey to a grinding halt.

If youth knew and age could, like my granddad often said, *the world would be a different place.*

Mike, Rohit and I exchanged silent glances. And we did it repeatedly that day, just so the younglings wouldn't get worried. My mind was abuzz with the ferocity of someone who had not caved in so far and not allowed anything or anyone to thwart our last picnic in Tawang. Yet here we were. And I was livid.

Damn you! We're going to go around you, just you watch!

I craned my neck up and looked at the mountain on our side. It was at a near ninety-degree incline and approximately fifty feet from the road above. Two things were clear: We could no longer follow the stream or scale the vertical slope to reach the road above.

All right, fine! Maybe not go around you then! But damn you!

This was a spanner in the works but there were two ways ahead: We could either 'abort mission' and head back the same way, conceding defeat. Pragmatism, good sense and Mike – all insisted that was the wise thing to move. Or, we could cross the waters and walk along the other side to reach the Red Bridge.

P.S. By the time that fateful day ended, I remember how much I'd wished better sense had prevailed. But if 'abort mission' had ever been a real option for me, this tale wouldn't be worth telling, would it?

15

ROHIT: *THAT'S NEARLY THREE TIMES THE WIDTH.*

Gigi: *Where is Bhalu?*

Mike: *We don't have the proper gear but ...*

Neha: *Okay, Didi, let's do it.*

Mona: *I. am. NOT. stepping. in. first.*

Me: *We just came out of an adventure camp, remember?*

And there was silence ...

With that exchange, it was settled. We were going to cross the approximately thirty-feet-wide rivulet and continue our onwards 'expedition'.

I have sketchy memories of the exact arguments for or against the brave new plan but my word prevailed. Perhaps it was my infinite belief that nothing could go wrong that made everyone comply. I don't recall the timid Mona resisting either. If she did, it would've been an inner monologue at best.

I've understood that people want something to believe in, someone with conviction to follow. And they want it so bad that very often, they will follow the Pied Piper to the proverbial edge of the cliff. All arguments against my idea to cross the water couldn't hold water (no pun intended). At thirteen, I had no fears of any kind. The five sensed my conviction and put their faith in it.

That handled, I looked at the waters with an arrogant glint in my eye. *I don't fear you, my watery friend!*

What a marvellous feeling that is. Fearlessness. It's a darn drug. The belief that no harm can ever come to you, that you have got nothing to lose, that you are basically invincible, it can be a very strong and potent propeller. I have had this feeling many times since. Sometimes it has worked beautifully and when it hasn't, I've licked my wounds for a few days, then dusted myself off and started over. Rocky Balboa's 'It ain't about how hard you hit, it's about how hard you can get hit and keep moving forward' is an absolute truth and plays on auto-repeat inside my head. Thank you, Mr Sly!

As I got everyone to agree to the new course of action, I recall thinking that I wouldn't let 'them' win. 'Them' being the powers that had been playing truant from the very start of the day. The chaperone ditching us, the vehicle breaking down and the walking path being devoured by the water. Someone or something did not want us to go on this picnic. And it was having a field day, the sadist! I wondered why it had to be this way? I think I do know better now but in that moment, I had many theories, mostly of the side-splitting kind.

Was Loki, the Norse god of fire and primary mischief-maker, playing games with us? Creating futile obstacles? Was he challenging me and smirking sadistically whilst doing so? My thirteen-year-old self would have wanted a duel to settle the matter (and obviously lost). Not without a fight, though. At the time, however, I believed I simply could not lose.

I remembered a quote from *King Lear*, 'As flies to wanton boys, are we to the Gods; they kill us for their sport.' *How could Shakespeare write something so terribly unfair and pin the blame on God*, I'd wondered.

So there they were: the two probable culprits. Loki and/or Shakespeare. The blame lay somewhere between The Avengers *and* King Lear. *While I couldn't have been bothered to waste time explaining to the stuffy old Bard how absolutely wrong he was in judging God, I certainly had plans when it came to Loki.*

'Let's use these sticks,' Mike said calmly while I was mentally preparing for that grand imaginary duel, bugle playing in the background, military style. My inner monologue interrupted and the three of us started to yank thin branches off the shrubs nearby. We checked them for strength by bending and pulling at both ends. This was the land of 'false vegetation' after all. We checked for length too, keeping the width of the waters we intended to cross in mind.

As per Rohit's calculation, we'd need branches at least three to four feet in length. Gigi tittered as I checked a few branches for length, using her as my stadiometer. Gigi was our human scale. The pigtailed little Gigi's giggles put a smile on all our faces. That's the face I remember.

I recently came across a black-and-white GIF of a little girl in a white nightdress and mop of curls on her head. The girl in the GIF giggled just like Gigi, making it my favourite GIF. Little Gigi would be etched in my memories of Tawang forever.

So, here was the plan.

Rohit, Mike and I would form a human chain in the water, connected to each other with reed-like branches. Gigi, Neha and Mona would cross the rivulet in that order, using the three of us as a bridge, holding on to us and the branches. Once they had crossed the water, the three of us would cross over together.

As soon as the right type of branches were procured, we went over the plan one last time.

Rohit, the tallest among us, would step into the water first, his branch in hand. Mike would hold the far end of that branch and go next followed by me.

To save my hoodie from getting soaked, I took it off and tied it around my shoulders. Mike and Rohit, who were taller, kept theirs on. 'You must have your hands free and mind completely focused during the crossing,' I said, while taking away the food bags in Mona's and Neha's hands and placing them with mine.

'Gigi goes first, followed by Neha and finally Mona,' I added. It was only logical to transport everyone in ascending order of height. Move the youngest and most vulnerable to safety first.

As Rohit stepped into the water, I experienced a severe case of butterflies in the stomach. The good doctor had said that when you got nervous, a nerve in the gut got activated, causing the fluttering sensation in the stomach. My gut was waving a red flag in my face. That apart, my heart was racing too.

P.S. The next thirty minutes are carved in my memory in stone. There is no escaping them and I have often visualized a dozen difference scenarios since. In all of those mental simulations, I end up a complete wreck for the rest of my life or dead at thirteen.

16

'THE WATER IS REALLY COLD!'

While we had expected the water to be chilly, its depth took us by surprise. Rohit had rolled his pants up to his knees to keep them from getting wet. *Ah, well!*

He waded further into the water and, within a few minutes, the water had risen up to his thighs. I wonder now if he had been calculating the depth as he went along. I suspect the other four were watching his river-walk with just as much trepidation.

Slow and cautious, Rohit stumbled for a moment but was quick to regain balance. Fluttering butterflies again! I was jittery. Maybe for the first time that day. After he had advanced five feet into the rivulet, Rohit pivoted on his foot to turn back and extend the branch to Mike, who stepped in next.

I didn't bother rolling my olive-green pants up. It was futile given how deep the water ran in some areas. The truth was that we had simply not factored in a river-crossing in our plan. Or, having to trudge in soggy jungle boots and pants for the rest of the day. But if this was the only way forward, so be it. We had to adapt. *Although the continual squeaking of the wet boots would be annoying*, I thought to myself.

Adjusting the bag of food and other supplies on my shoulder, I beamed at the girls with absolute confidence, 'This is so much fun, right? The river-walk, river-crossing and then we picnic by the Red Bridge with sandwiches, juice and yummy mango slices.' Gigi and Neha seemed to imagine the scenario, looking excited. Mona smiled too. I guessed the team morale was fine. I only had to maintain mine.

Turning my attention back to the boys, I held onto the branch extended by Mike and stepped in. Rohit had reached three fourths across the rivulet; Mike was three feet in too. The human bridge was nearly ready for use and that fluttering sensation in my gut started surging again.

I'd never let slip from memory what the water taught me that day. It's one thing to sense there's trouble ahead but a whole other thing to experience it.

The water felt freezing cold. I would acclimatize to it quickly and so would the others, I reasoned internally. But there was a bigger problem at hand, one that my small frame couldn't find a way around.

This new complication, I suppose, was simple to describe: a deceptively strong current. What had mostly looked harmless on the surface was anything but that!

The absolute treachery! Loki had tricked me after all.

With my heart thumping like a jackhammer, I waded in deeper. Crossing the rivulet had seemed much easier in theory. As I pushed through the current and took the next step gingerly, I was thinking about Neha, Gigi and Mona. Would they be able to cross despite the bridge we had created for them? I shut down the thought immediately and focused on the job at hand.

Trying to walk in a straight line in running water is a lot harder than it looks. Even in a swimming pool, you must push hard against the moving current.

Imagine the force of water in a rivulet flowing down a mountain. Imagine the crushing pressure it exerts on anything that potentially comes in its way. We were in its way.

Now add a landmine of slippery stones and gravel generously spread across its entire bed.

Whatever you have imagined, it was three times harder for six children.

As I took my next step in the raging waters, yes it felt like rage, I slipped and fell. I still recall Neha's terrified call as I fell. Fortunately, the water wasn't very deep and I had held on tightly to Mike's branch. He was strong enough to keep his balance. While I got back on my feet quickly, I was soaked to the bone, including my hoodie and the food bags – which by some stroke of luck – were still on my shoulder. *Surely the tight covers of the stainless steel tiffins would save the food inside.*

Not to be deterred, I continued moving forward. Lifting my foot, I sliced through the current with twice the strength whilst gingerly making contact with the rocky riverbed. An instinctive – almost reflective strategy – to stay on my feet.

The devil was not unknown anymore, so to speak. But the damage was done. Gigi had started to bawl, dampening our collective frame of mind.

P.S. I learnt that day that you must never underrate a seemingly placid adversary. And if that foe is water, then you have been duly warned. Water bodies in the mountains can be deceiving! It might look like comely rivulets prancing and cooing sweet gurgling nothings, but they can sweep you off your feet, and not in that beguiling, fallacious sort of way. Their innate rage and brute force will find the path of least resistance. And only the mighty Lord can contain them!

Interestingly, five years back, I had gone for a river-walk on the outskirts of Mumbai. Seemingly a walk in the park for me, right? But when I stepped into the placid-looking river and grabbed the rope to cross it, my muscle memory kicked in, along with the full knowledge of deceptive currents and slippery riverbeds. While it momentarily made my heart thump wildly, the water also brought back what I'd learnt. So I pushed my foot hard into the riverbed while grabbing the rope with all my strength and crossed it. I understood water better now. In the middle of the shallow but raging river were a few rapids but I was the only one in the group to make it to the other side, without floundering or an untoward event.

Common sense demands that you know your enemy well before you charge into battle. Not everyone though will apply the aforementioned wisdom before a 'charge'. Truthfully, I did not know how to swim when I stepped into those waters that day. 'Tis true, fools do go where angels fear to tread.

Maybe the fearless are foolish …

17

ME: *COME ON, GIGI, LET US GO. THE WATER FEELS NICE.*

Mike: *The Red Bridge is right there, Gigi, look!*

Mona: *Bhalu is waiting for you Gigi, go baby …*

Neha: *I will gift you my best barbie, Gigi, go …*

Her face tear-streaked, little Gigi was clinging to Mona's leg and refusing to budge. An impasse we could ill afford.

'I'll cross,' Neha said collectedly and stepped into the water. My little sister's courage, coupled with her unshakeable faith in me, came with colossal responsibility. I instantly put my branch out, 'Hold it tightly, walk very slowly and do not let go of the branch.' Neha followed instructions to the T, slowly reached my spot. I breathed easy.

'The water is just a little deeper, but you'll do fine, hold on to Mike's branch,' I instructed, while watching her like a hawk. Neha waded past me, holding onto Mike's branch.

'You're doing great, Neha, keep going,' Mike called out loudly as she got closer to the centre of the rivulet.

For a moment or two, I saw her legs shaking in the current and it was nerve-wracking. With my heart in my mouth, I supressed my quivering voice and muttered: 'Good.' I was fumbling for words.

Neha's walk across the river felt excruciatingly long. Like a rubber band stretched to its limits.

It is peculiar how moments of happiness and euphoria seem to pass over like greased lightning when compared to the ones filled with pain or anxiety. I often ask myself if happiness is genuinely fleeting or if we are hardwired to believe that human beings are born to suffer, and for that very reason tend to sadistically amplify and stretch our anxieties? Could our age-old conditioning be in cahoots with Loki? Maybe, maybe not. I am still debating this, internally.

Every muscle in my body was stiff with tension. Neha was shorter than me and lighter too. Aware of the odds, I said a silent prayer. Would she be able to withstand the current? Her successful river crossing was the test of my plan. I never doubted the plan; it was the only way forward. But by then, I also knew a plan need not necessarily go the way you wanted it to.

'Gigi! Look, the water is fine,' Neha turned back and shouted as she reached Mike. Whilst still clinging to Mona, Gigi was sullen but watching intently.

My heartbeat racing, I intervened agitatedly, 'Neha don't turn back, don't talk, don't leave the branch. Slow and steady, keep going.' Neha immediately sensed my anxiety and plodded on. She was always quick to pick up on someone's mood and respond with rare sensitivity. I was on tenterhooks. I could not allow my younger sibling to get distracted or falter.

She was in waist-deep water now and, according to my calculation, maybe two feet away from Rohit. That is when it started to drizzle.

You have got to be kidding me, Lord.

Trying hard to keep my nerves under check, I egged Neha on, hoping she had not noticed it yet but who was I fooling! We all heard Gigi's, 'It's raining, look!'

Neha turned to look at me, her large, expressive eyes speaking volumes – imploring, a little unsure. She wanted to know what to do next.

'Keep going, it's just a drizzle, don't turn back,' I said keeping my voice firm.

Lord let her cross safely, please Lord!

Mike shot me a look. The calm and gentle Mike, whom I had thrust in the middle of the rivulet and this unplanned adventure, half smiled at me. It was his way of telling me to relax. But how could I? He had not taken the decisions I had. The onus, if anything were to go wrong today, was mine. This was my burden to bear. My job was to pull through and, at that particular moment, it was only about crossing the water. Given my precarious predicament, I just couldn't smile back.

Rohit looked at Neha calmly, 'Come, you're almost there.' While my mind was abuzz again, my eyes followed every step of hers and, as she set foot on the ground finally, I whooped with joy and sent out a silent prayer of gratitude.

Thank you, Lord!

She had made it across. We all would too.

Regaining my composure and taking a deep breath, I turned to the two girls and smiled. 'Who is next?'

Gigi thrust her hand up in the air, like an enthusiastic child eager to please the teacher. 'Me,' she squealed with excitement.

What a relief that was!

But before Gigi could step into the water, the drizzle turned into a blinding downpour. Within seconds, heavy rain started falling in slants, forcing me to shut my eyes and plant my feet firmly. The sounds of the Jungle were disrupted by the boom of thunder while drops fell like bullets, covering all surrounding foliage and feeling like pin pricks on my face.

'Wait there,' I motioned loudly to Mona to hold Gigi back. We had to wait until the train cleared out a bit.

The ominous clouds had come out of nowhere and smothered the sun, killing its light. The rivulet had turned a muggy shade of grey as the raindrops violently punctured the surface of the water. Mona and Gigi took cover, as did Neha. There was enough rock and foliage around but the rest of us were exposed to the elements. The sudden boom of thunder that rocked the dark skies did not help either. *This was a darn mess!*

I raced through our options. What if the weather packed up for good and the water started to dangerously rise and swell up? It would be impossible to stand in the water, let alone have anyone cross it. Importantly, Mike, Rohit and I would have to decide which side to cross over to. With Neha on one side and Gigi and Mona on the other, there was no easy answer.

P.S. And none of us saw the mudslide coming.

18

FOR FIVE LONG MINUTES, THE SKIES RUMBLED AND POURED, carpet-bombing the Jungle with spear-like drops. Puncturing the surface of the water with ferocity and purpose, those dark clouds were unrelenting. Unleashing their little warrior drops with the express purpose of drowning us. Cooking up a storm, relishing the deluge. Or perhaps the clouds were not at fault; maybe their delicate frame could no longer hold the water. Maybe the Jungle had conspired with Zeus and Indra.

The downpour was so intense, walking through a waterfall could not have got us any wetter.

It was one thing to wait it out by the side and a whole other thing to be in the middle of the waters while the rain and the Jungle were conniving to twist the knife further. I had had enough. I felt the water around me swell and rise, making the current stronger than when we had waded in. There was a definite conspiracy to do us in!

Digging my heels into the rocky bed, I stood resolute. Mike and Rohit were holding their ground too. We had decided to stay put. Squinting my eyes to avoid being blinded by the rain, I looked up at those black-as-the-night tufts in the sky; those nasty fellows busy, obliterating the sun and bringing darkness to the valley.

What timing, you guys! There is a god above, you know that, right? (Ah, well.)

Maybe there was an instinct and an understanding of the weather in Tawang. Ever-changing, whimsical and eccentric. Maybe it was a prayer borne out of indignant exasperation. The downpour ended as abruptly as it had begun so I suppose my instinct was right. Nothing lasts forever. The skies cleared out and all was well with the world again.

'Come on, Gigi, let us go,' I said, wiping the water off my face. We had to move quickly. We could not risk another curveball in our way.

Gigi dug her heels in and clung tightly to Mona.

'Come, we'll quickly cross and then enjoy picnic time with Milkmaid and sandwiches,' I goaded her while hinting at the goodies in my soggy shoulder bag. 'Bhalu is waiting for you this side, Gigi, come!' Neha added, hoping our furry companion would do the trick.

'I want to go home,' Gigi whined and plopped down. I looked at Mona with urgency but said nothing. We had to start moving and Mona knew it.

'Go, Gigi, it's fine. I am right behind you,' Mona said reassuringly.

Just like that and without warning, a large chunk of earth came sliding down, right behind Mona and Gigi. Shrubs with mud still clinging to its roots in thick wet clumps, little rocks and loose mud had slid down the side of the mountain and landed right at the edge of the waters. A big messy heap of a near-disaster fell inches away from the two.

Reflexively, Mona lifted Gigi up in her arms and stepped away quickly.

Neha shrieked. We were so busy goading Gigi to cross that none of us saw it coming. What would have happened if that chunk of earth had slid and dropped straight into the waters with all that force! Would Mike, Rohit and I been able to hold our ground?

'Take her,' Mona said decisively and pushed a crying Gigi towards me. There was no time to waste. The region was known for landslides and the ensuing wrath of nature. Even adults would not survive if a chunk of earth buried them or worse, swept them away with the water; what chance did the six of us have? None really.

Gigi looked at me like a deer in the headlights. She had frozen after taking her first step into the water. 'Come, Gigi, one more step,' I cajoled, but to no end. Gigi refused to budge.

'Go, Gigi,' Mona goaded with urgency as smaller chunks of loose earth continued to fall from the mountainside. There was no time to lose.

'Gigi, we have to picnic at the Red Bridge,' Neha repeated with urgency.

But she took another step and froze again. It was both frustrating and frightening. At this rate, we were sitting ducks, waiting for another disaster to strike us. I took a quick decision.

Releasing Mike's stick and flinging mine into the water, I stretched my entire body out and tried to reach her.

'Look at me, Gigi,' I said as firmly and gently as was possible. 'Come, we have to go now.'

'Go, Gigi,' Mona shouted. Everyone was a little impatient, their nerves on edge.

I dug my heels into the rocky bed and pushed my hand as far as it could go. Stretching out every inch of myself, I grabbed Gigi's hand and smiled reassuringly. 'Come now,' I said. The harried Gigi started to move and took two quick steps towards me.

While it was exasperating for us to cajole her, I can only imagine a six-year-old's state of mind. Terrified down to the last cell in her body. This was supposed to be a straightforward, fun yet uneventful picnic by the Red Bridge. And here she was, being made to cross, what would have looked like the fiercest of rivers. Little Gigi had not signed up for an adventure that had been wilfully thrust upon her, by me.

Grabbing Gigi's little arm with both my hands, I started to pull her closer. She was too short to stay above the water so the sticks would come in handy. That was the plan and while we had factored in for height and size, especially Gigi's, I simply hadn't factored in for what happens when fear cripples a child.

As soon as Gigi reached me in the water, I took away my right hand to grab Mike's stick. Big mistake!

Gigi saw me release her from my right hand, panicked and started to thrash about, her eyes filled with fear.

'Gigi, I am still holding you, I won't let you go, Gigi, don't worry!' I said, trying to calm her frayed nerves while grabbing Mike's branch. But Gigi, who was bobbing in the water, was not listening. If she were an adult, one could have said she had a panic attack. It might have been easy to reason with an adult in a similar situation but not with such a young child. A fearful six-year-old is just that – a six-year-old in a dither.

And then it happened. Gigi slipped out of my hands.

Until that fateful moment, I did not quite understand the anatomy of fear. Creeping up surreptitiously, it could permeate your skin and, before you knew it, course through your veins like a tidal wave. A thumping heart and a parched mouth were classic symptoms of surrender. With the rational side of the brain hijacked, fear could paralyse you at will or compel you to jump out of your skin when you most needed to stay calm. Standing in those raging waters, I learnt that fear most certainly could also kill.

Gigi had thrashed her arms and legs so violently that I lost my balance and fell, and, in that moment, she slipped out of my grip. And before anyone could react, the little girl was swept downstream.

It happened in a split second, but its memory will last an eternity. I can conjure it at will even to this day. And for good reason.

P.S. Gigi, wherever you are, if you read this: You taught me my greatest lesson. In many ways, watching you slip away became a reality check and it also revealed to me who I was and who I needed to be.

19

NEHA WAS CRYING OUT FOR HELP. I WAS TOLD LATER THAT Mona was screaming too. But I do not recall hearing anything but the sound of my own heartbeat, every single pound in my chest. Thumping and drowning everything else out. The world outside had become a big blur. Without thinking or perhaps even breathing, I flung Mike's branch into the water and leapt in after Gigi.

This was not a decision, a strategy or even a counter-measure of some sort. Every cell in my body moved with an instinctive force that is hard to explain. I suppose you don't really contemplate in such moments. Your body simply surrenders to your gut or perhaps your strongest impulse.

I was also told that I had leapt into the water like someone possessed and it had all happened in a flash. While I don't recall my physical reaction to losing Gigi in great detail, I can still summon my emotional response to this day. The cacophonous thrumming rhythm inside my chest and echoing in my ears. Duh-duhn! Duh-duhn! All hell had broken loose, and the world was ending. It really did feel like the end.

No! No! No! No! No!

Having thrown myself into the running current, I pushed down hard against the slippery riverbed with deep desperation. I was trying to propel myself and gain some momentum. While Gigi was in my line of sight, she was out of reach and being washed away faster than I could reach her. It was a different matter that I hadn't learnt how to swim yet and had no inkling of the depth and currents that lay ahead.

Like a ragdoll, little Gigi was being swept away. I saw her pigtails and screamed after her a few times, gulping water and coughing violently each time I tried. *Stupid!* Why was I screaming? What did I hope to achieve? It wasn't like Gigi would stop, turn around and run to me or listen to my shouts. She was helpless, her arms in the air, flaying about. I was struggling to wade, slipping and being swept away by the fierce current. It had the upper hand and I had little control on my movement. Defying the current was impossible.

Gigi was a few feet ahead when I remember falling into a hole or a pit in the rivulet bed. That thump and muffled beating of my heart as I slipped under! Every cell in my body was jolted by the sudden fall. I gulped in – what felt like a bucketload of water – trying to furiously thrash my way up. I had never been this terrified and overwhelmed.

This kind of suffocation is hard to describe. As you gasp for air but all you do is ingest more water. You gasp till you can gasp no more. It is hard to think straight when you are this utterly powerless and yet this is when your instinct for the self-preservation instinct kicks in.

Tread if you can't swim, gently tread. And relax, do not panic.

In that moment of deep distress, I heard my father's voice. My heard was still thumping wildly but for a brief moment, I stopped flaying my arms violently and fighting the water. I let my body relax. Perhaps, I surrendered to it …

As I tried to calm myself, my body came up for air.

Providentially, it was just one pit and my feet found the riverbed again. But the water current was too strong for me to keep my balance. I was constantly going under and frantically flaying my arms and legs to try staying afloat. It was impossible not to panic. Gigi was a few feet ahead of me when I lunged for her. But I couldn't. My fingers merely grazed her clothes as she slipped away.

Before we knew it, the two of us were swept around the mountain that had banked left.

Oh, please, God, please! Please, please!

As I pushed my arms out to move fast towards Gigi, I saw water frothing just a few metres ahead. There they were. Rapids, and we were about to hit them.

Rapids meant greater water turbulence, lesser control and very high chances of colliding into rocks in the water. And what of the injuries? The rapids did scare me. They still do.

I thrashed harder and with urgent desperation. I had to save her, I had to save me. Gigi was a few feet away from the start of the rapids when, I believe, the universe or God or some higher power, intervened.

Just ahead of us was an old tree growing out the side of the mountain, a thick mangled branch bent over the water, a few feet above the surface.

What was it? An instinctive reflex or sheer luck or something else. Its branch was crooked like an arm, leaning in. That tree was my only chance.

Leaping into the air with the last bit of strength I had left, I lunged for Gigi and grabbed the edge of her hoodie. This time, my fingers had unyielding purpose and a will of their own. With Gigi held tightly in my grasp, I stretched my left arm out to grab the old branch. It was a foot or so away.

Come on, come on!

Pushing against the current with all my might, I moved diagonally towards the tree, holding on to Gigi for dear life.

Come on! Come on! One more step!

My heart was still beating like a drum. We inched closer to the tree and finally our downstream drift in the waters came to a halt.

Duh-duhn duh-duhn duh-duhn …

And just like that, the death-by-drowning headline changed to being rescued by an old tree.

Trees listen, especially old ones. Of that I am sure. And long before *Avatar* made the sacred 'Tree of Souls' on Pandora popular, I had inadvertently experienced a powerful neural connection with an old tree in the jungles of Tawang, whose age and rot had probably made it lean over the water.

The old fellow had put his hand out to save us and defied the Jungle in doing so.

Holding on to the proverbial olive branch that the universe had extended in the very nick of time, Gigi and I bobbed in the waters together. Despite the loud gushing of the rivulet, a bizarre silence descended upon me, the echoes of my heart beating slowly became duller. My face flushed and I felt a strange chill. That's when I heard Bhalu barking and saw Neha running along the other side on the bank. Her face ashen and panic-stricken. Breathless and coughing, I motioned a thumbs-up to her. Neha ran back to inform the others.

If there was ever a lull after a storm, this was it. For the first time since the start of that day, I felt I was done. Overwhelmed and somewhat crushed. Stunned, I shivered, my arm tightly wrapped around Gigi's middle. Coughing and wanting to cry.

The rescue had taken place just as suddenly as Gigi slipping out of my hands. Was it pure coincidence that I was born left-handed and the old tree that saved us was on the left side of the rivulet?

As Mike and Rohit fished us out, I remember feeling my knees buckle as my legs touched the ground. Neha rushed to me and held me tightly, her whole body shaking. She was in shock.

Mona crossed over with Rohit's help, grabbed Gigi and hugged her. Mike was thumping my back hard, to aid in expectorating the water I had glugged. Gigi was coughing too while Mona thumped her back. Our lungs had survived but we were a mess. Perhaps like me, she too was reeling under the weight of our shared experience in hell. Neha was holding onto me, her eyes filled with tears and relief.

Feeling powerless and overwhelmed by the near drowning, my entire energy had been sapped.

I sank down on a rock. My whole body was trembling. Taking off my jungle boots to drain out the water, I saw the Victorinox hunter knife fall out. When we started out, I had tucked it into the side of the boot in a tiny flat pocket. Miraculously, the water hadn't claimed it, like it had my hoodie. Holding the knife in my hand, and feeling its sharp edges with my quivering fingers, I looked at the water. I hugged Neha. I was in shock too.

And it struck me like a bolt. We could have drowned. The water had taken both Gigi and me. Importantly, my choices had backfired and brought me and another child to the brink of death.

My memories after the near-drowning are blurry but even after all this time, I still remember what I had said to Mike. With urgency and steely resolve, fighting back a barrage of emotions.

'Whatever happens to us today, we live or we die, we have to save these little ones.'

P.S. Held on to dear life by the skin of one's teeth. The idiom is near impossible to explain to someone who has not experienced it. I remember watching a tsunami-survival movie headlined by a famous Hollywood actor. As she was being swept away, in the largest water-tank set ever built for a movie, the fear in her eyes was real. All too real and familiar. Maybe because, as she had confessed during the promotions, she didn't know how to swim.

You cannot fake that kind of fear. You cannot explain it, either. We see things like this in the movies and believe that's where they belong, and that all fiction comes out of a writer's imagination. But all good reels often follow the real and truth is usually far stranger than fiction. Ever since that picnic, I've been inexorably drawn to man-versus-nature survival stories, vicariously wanting to relive the rush I felt that day. Often, I have screamed exasperatedly, 'Don't do it, you'll get yourself killed,' just as the people in those stories are about to make a stupid move. But more importantly, *to remind myself that I survived … we had survived.*

Adrenaline junkies, I tell you, they never learn!

20

THE NEAR-DROWNING EXPERIENCE SHIFTED SOMETHING inside me. I fell into a peculiar kind of silence, the kind that leads to deeper revelations and connects you with your own self. My limbs were still trembling from the debacle and while I was grateful that we had not ended up dead, I knew this was a warning call.

It fell like a sledgehammer or was it my mother's voice inside my head? I'm not quite sure but I understood that one's innocuous decisions could have consequences. Catastrophic consequences. Mine had put everyone in harm's way.

Often a seemingly well-thought-through choice or action can set into motion a series of unexpected events that can further snowball and metamorphize that first action into a Frankenstein's monster, which can no longer be controlled.

Often the unexpected turn of events can lead us to dead ends. And those dead ends will undoubtedly compel us to make more choices, sometimes even worse ones. So it all boils down to the one simple truth. That at the end of it all, the first choice we made will be the only one we will really get to make. The rest is just Loki playing games with you.

Too morbid? Maybe so, but factoring in for curveballs of all sorts and sizes and making peace with the idea of the domino effect will save our sorrys selves from getting scarred, crushed and whatever else. It will hopefully enable us to take more calculated risks. Knowing that our actions have real-world consequences could also make us choose wisely in the first instance.

This was a very harsh lesson for a thirteen-year-old and a tad unfair at the time.

I had convinced the five to get off the road and follow the stream. It was another means to an end. The Red Bridge. At the time, it had seemed a harmless decision. Couldn't I have just gotten away with it? Could it not have been a pleasurable walk to the Red Bridge, the six of us happily cackling, taking pictures, gorging on mango slices and Milkmaid-sweetened sandwiches? Could it not have been a memorable picnic day and a perfect parting gift from Tawang to us?

It was the perfect parting gift, but it has taken me years to wrap my head around it.

In that moment, as I dragged myself out of the waters, my trigger-happy days were over. The brazenness of teen-induced bravado washed away. This was no longer a peachy picnic trail. My inherent confidence was quickly and quietly replaced by the need to survive. I was not risk averse, only more aware of the ensuing consequences.

We had to make it back alive. Regardless of curveballs, sledgehammers and other instruments of shock and awe.

We had to save ourselves from the devious Loki's tricks! It was all about survival now.

P.S. The rivulet cost us all our food and essential supplies. When I lunged after Gigi to save her, I was holding mine, Mona's and Neha's shoulder bags. We had carefully split the food supplies between us that morning. Turns out, it was a wasteful exercise. At the moment of reckoning, the bags were the last thing on my mind.

In the aftermath, let me say that we were in very deep trouble! The sandwiches, canned mango slices, Tang, tea, biscuits, Milkmaid, compass were all gone. The camera had been washed away, too. The watch on my wrist wasn't waterproof, so it had met a watery end as well.

Three raincoats, a few bottles of water and the Ziplock with basic first aid. That's all that was left because they were in Rohit's and Mike's bags.

The water took away more than my confidence and pride. It took away our means to survive the Jungle.

21

SOMETIMES YOU HAVE TO CHOOSE BETWEEN THE DEVIL AND the deep blue sea. If experience has taught me anything, it is this – whatever you choose, it will damn you and define you in equal parts. Also, no choice will ever come without riders.

As time has passed, I've also come to acknowledge how absolutely marvellous that is! How a set of choices that lead two different kinds of people down the same rabbit hole can give them their own unique paths. Each journey as surprising as the inherent beauty in that paradox. And yet if you were to simply connect the dots, it will all add up. Always.

At the time, however, there seemed only one prudent option. The rivulet, as we had witnessed first-hand, could not be trusted to guide us to our destination anymore. The sneaky, conniving brute had all but done us in. For a change, it would be a real relief to have solid ground beneath our feet whilst finding our way to the Red Bridge, or a road back to civilization. We didn't need any fresh trouble the waters could tsunami our way. The Jungle was a safer bet.

And as far from the water as possible!

I took my next decision, yes this was mine too, much more thought through, and it received a thumping approval from the five, who were still pretty shaken up. I was surprised by their faith despite all that had transpired. Although, they saw the incident differently from me.

In their version, Gigi panicked, thrashed about, slipped out of my hands and got swept away. If it hadn't been for me, who rescued her despite no swimming skills, she'd be dead. *It was not surprising from someone who had won the greatest number of trophies at the adventure camp,* it was reasoned. It was an unsettling amount of pressure, but it propelled me further.

In my version, however, I was the villain of the piece. I had put them all in harm's way and risked the life of the youngest member of the erstwhile picnic party. A picnic it no longer was and a hero I certainly was not.

If Gigi and I had drowned, I shudder to imagine what would have happened to the ones left behind. Would they have given up?

Thankfully, we had both survived so the *what if* became far more morbid and terrifying. Invincibility was now a rapidly vanishing delusion. The Jungle had humbled me.

My takeaway from the near-drowning was that one can survive most setbacks in the physical realm if one survives it in their subconsciousness. The very illusion of invincibility that had put me in harm's way had also saved me. In my mind, at no point did the waters kill my spirit or my fight to save Gigi. The need to save Gigi had displaced all fear.

On the subject of survival, I want to share a case in point from boxing and golf. In boxing, long before your come to blows with your opponent, sometimes long before you enter the ring, and often, while you wait in your corner, you know how the fight will go. Because you've either visualized delivering that brutal upper cut or seen yourself hitting the canvas, knocked out. You just know in your gut.

The same applies to golf. You can only cross a water hazard if you do not see it. It is oddly simple. In your mind, the hazard must not exist. That is the key to crossing it.

A few years after the said picnic, it took me thirty swings to cross a water hazard at a golf course in Delhi. The golf-crazed Korean threesome behind me, who were paying a fortune to play the eighteen holes twice, wanted to fling their clubs at me in frustration, for holding them up. It was only after my experienced caddy shared the magic mantra that I was able to cross it. The mantra was: If the problem did not exist in your mind, it would not exist at all. It was all in the mind. Victory and defeat.

Guess the *water hazard* from that fateful day in Tawang remained hazardous for a long time to come.

Over the next few years, I bumped into Mike and Mona in two different cantonments. Oddly, I seemed to remember that day the most vividly. They recalled key highlights while I could recall it blow by blow. Gasp by gasp.

It was not only because I was leading the group and making all the decisions, but because I believed it was my cross to bear. It was my journey. That adventure was meant to reveal who I was, and my acute sense of self-awareness stems from all that transpired on that day in Tawang. I also think misadventures, much like failures, are powerful inflection points and must be given their rightful place under the sun. They have a great hand in steering us onto the path that's right for us.

I stared blankly into the Jungle as we were about to enter it.

P.S. The Jungle stared back … and threw open its arms. Open like the magnificent Venus flytrap.

22

A JUNGLE IS A BEAST. AS IS A MOUNTAIN. TOGETHER, THEY are a formidable adversary. If you are planning to lose your way or undertake a survival course, you do not want to be doing it in a jungle spread across hundreds of miles of mountainous terrain. Not unless you're in the Special Forces. And definitely not if you are a child.

But here we were, facing the lesser of the two evils, hopefully.

The plan was straightforward, at least in my mind. Climb the mountain, get to a vantage point and, from those heights, spot the Red Bridge and descend on it. It was a circuitous route but it was the only way to avoid the water. It was a whole other matter that we had no food, navigation sense or chaperone, let alone any equipment or real knowledge to sustain or guide us.

The Jungle, with its wild sylvan utopia, looked appealing and tangible. We were surrounded by viridescent bliss in all directions, and the crisp air tasted sweet and fresh. The synchronic feeling of being inconsequential and belonging meshed into one heady fantasy. The Jungle evoked myriad emotions.

The sun was almost overhead when the six of us entered the Jungle. Seven actually. Bhalu had joined us, having reappeared as suddenly as he'd gone missing in action. Gigi, who'd been quiet all this while, lit up upon seeing our furry companion. Genuinely relieved, I marvelled at the speed with which the six-year-old had flicked the switch on the recent trauma, like the antiquated telephone exchange back in the day where the plug would be pulled out from one socket to put into another. And just like that, it was a whole new conversation. Gigi's mental chatter changed course with Bhalu's appearance. As did Neha's who was holding my hand tight. My protective younger sister wanted to ensure I didn't do anything perilous.

As Gigi got chatty with Bhalu, I turned my attention to the path ahead of us. The rustle of the trees, the birdcalls, the sounds of crickets filled my senses. If there were any predatory creatures, they were well camouflaged, and you would never know they were there unless you were their chosen quarry for the day!

The Jungle was throbbing with life. Peppered with an uneven canopy of trees of varying sizes, it had a distinct bottle-green hue – the effect of the lush hue of vitality and life that arrives on the wings of clouds bursting with rain and a cool summer. There was life in every direction. I distinctly remember it – alpine shrubs, climbers, trees with broad leaves and the coniferous kind, growing together in clusters and bizarrely shaped flowers, which I later discovered are called orchids. These oddly shaped, brilliant-coloured flowers that sold at a steep premium in the cities, were growing in abundance in the wild.

There were also naked rock features strewn across the terrain and bursting forth from the surface of the mountain, like icebergs. From the vantage of the jungle floor, it was not possible to see too far ahead; but if I'd had a bird's eye view, I would have seen a thick cluster of clouds floating across, blocking the sun entirely, and a whole lot more. Thankfully, I didn't have the advantage of a drone's eye view just yet.

'Let us climb in a straight row all the way to the top,' Rohit said quietly, to which everyone agreed.

With the sun nearly overhead, we had little time to make it to the bridge, wherever it was. It looked around 1000 hours or 1030 in the morning. We had to go by instinct and whatever knowledge we had of the terrain. By 1830 hours, the sun would definitely set, and we'd be lost forever. My watch might have stopped ticking, but time had not. Thankfully, the waters had sharpened my senses or perhaps set them right!

Arming ourselves with sticks or low-hanging branches that we'd yanked off shrubs and smaller trees, we set off. The sticks would aid us in climbing and clearing the way – our improvised jungle-made machetes to take on all that the Jungle could hurl at us.

A few metres into the ascent, I turned around and looked back at the babbling waters. How deceptive they'd turned out to be. Strangely, I had mixed feelings as we left it behind. But it was clear as crystal to me that we were going home today.

P.S. If I could hear the Jungle, I would've heard its whispers: 'Come now, chop chop!' *Then it would have thrown its head back and let out a guttural laugh.*

23

A SHRILL SOUND REVERBERATED THROUGH THE JUNGLE.

'What's that?' Neha whispered. We froze in our tracks. Was it a weird mating call of some bird of prey or a wild animal?

Tawang was home to a stunning array of flora and fauna but the indigenous tiger species of this region was considered long extinct. Not that it sounded like a tiger, but it didn't hurt to rule out the worst-case scenario first! We had, however, heard of snow leopards and other predators in the higher reaches.

Looking above, I scanned the trees, adding a soft 'keep moving' as the six of us started to ascend again. But what if there was indeed a leopard crouched on its haunches, watching us and waiting for an opportune moment to make a meal out of us? Would a motley group of younglings be able to escape a tree-climbing predator in a forest? Especially if it was looking for prey?

I had heard stories about leopards dragging away unattended little children, their mauled bodies being found days later in the jungle. Could there be anyone more 'unattended' than us?

After all, we were on the leopard's home turf. Sliding my hand into my boot, I discreetly pulled out the hunter knife I'd picked up at a small Army canteen in Tezpur. In case the leopard attacked, perhaps we'd have a fighting chance? *The utter naivety of it.*

But I had made a promise to myself: the young ones had to live, whatever it took.

The sound didn't repeat itself and I eased up knowing that panicking was futile. Bhalu looked unaffected and continued to walk alongside Gigi so I reckoned the mysterious sound was best ignored for now.

The walking sticks were turning out to be handy as the ascent got steeper and the terrain became erratic. With no human tracks or trails of any sort – and we certainly weren't experts at reading animal tracks – it was clear we were in uncharted territory.

The hunter knife still in hand, I looked at Mike. In a grand gesture, he smiled and stepped ahead of me, shielding me from whatever was coming our way. As we reached a steep edge, Mike stretched his hand out to hoist me up. Grabbing it eagerly, trying hard to not blush, I felt a flutter in my stomach and blood rush to my cheeks. What an embarrassing and dead giveaway!

A week ago, my father's man Friday, a quiet Assamese man named Saikia, who would go to his death for my father and vice versa, had caught us walking hand in hand. While

I had yanked my hand away almost immediately; Saikia had pretended to not have seen anything. But for the next few days, I was on tenterhooks and the episode hung like a sword over my head. Fortunately, our budding romance had not been reported at the time.

This morning, we were free to hold hands, even to kiss but the picnic had turned into a scramble for survival. The Jungle had changed everything. Romance in that moment meant making sure we survived.

The attraction survived for a whole year even at school, where we were inseparable until Mike's father inevitably got posted out. While the loved-up handwritten cards and calls continued, the feelings faded away.

Mike, if you do read this, we'll always have that summer in Tawang. And that Jungle. It will belong to both of us: an ode to our shared teenage years.

24

BHALU WAS BARKING FURIOUSLY AS WE REACHED A GRASSY meadow-like patch, drawing our attention to a large rock feature covered with a moss-like growth. We stopped in our tracks and I tightened my grip on the Victorinox. What could it be?

Out sauntered a yak.

If there ever was a woolly mammoth the equivalent of a bull, it was the yak. We had seen these mountain creatures near the Tawang Monastery at the adventure camp and near the Se-La Pass but never up close. We had even watched them dressed in costumes at the annual Tawang Festival but seeing one in the wild felt altogether different. It had probably broken away from its herd and was peacefully grazing, oblivious to the flutter its sudden appearance had caused.

There is something mythical about yaks, like they belong to another time, from hundreds of years ago, teleported here by accident. As they roam the cold mountains in search of food, they look like stocky bulls with handlebar horns, wearing full-length shaggy woollen jackets.

The fellow stared at us. We stared back. Nobody moved. It was an impasse.

'Is it going to attack us?' Mona wondered aloud.

It was a valid question. To a bunch of children unfamiliar with the creature, the animal looked fearsome. Like a bull, only larger and with horns that could skewer two adults in one go. 'Yaks are like cows,' Mike whispered. 'Let's go around it,' Rohit added softly, pointing to roughly forty degrees away from the yak's grazing position.

No one wanted to take the risk, just in case the fellow decided today was its day to charge and turn into kebab a few small humans. 'We hold hands and move quickly. But no running, no talking,' I added whilst hatching an escape plan mentally.

The yak is a fat fellow so maybe we could outrun it, I reasoned. *What if we ran in alternating directions? It wasn't a dinosaur, you fool. Wait, what if we played dead? Like they tell you to do in case you are accosted by a bear in the wild? Or, maybe run and climb a tree? Moron, never expose your backside to anything with horns.* My head was abuzz ... *The fellow would stick his horns up your posterior and then what would you sit on? All right, let's just walk quietly and get out of its way ...*

Good talk!

If there was technology to chronicle inner monologues, mine would have made for an audiobook titled the *Theatre of the Quaint and Absolutely Absurd.*

As we took a semicircular detour to avoid it, Gigi curled her nose and whispered, 'Yak milk shtinks!' evoking muffled chuckles from all of us. Neha nodded in agreement but kept silent.

'Shhh,' Mona added quickly as we tiptoed, lest we attracted undue attention from Mister Yak.

Yak milk was the only fresh milk available in the region. Yellowish in colour and viscous with a distinct odour, our options every morning were to drink yak milk or sweet condensed Milkmaid. It was clearly not popular with the brats but was a huge source of nutrition and livelihood for the nomadic folk who bred these high-altitude creatures.

'Remember the yak butter lamps at the monastery?' I pointed out, recalling a visit from a few weeks ago. Mike and Neha nodded. 'Those little monks have such rosy cheeks. What do they eat?' Neha asked, transporting us all back to the Tawang Monastery. During the adventure camp, we had visited the monastery on a tour and watched the pint-sized monks in their maroon robes and sleeveless jackets with admiration. Most of them were under the age of ten; their cherry-tinted cheeks flushed with the heat as they dutifully poured and lit yak butter earthen lamps around the stunning Buddha idol that towered over the entire hall. It was a surreal sight that made everyone fall silent in awe.

In fact, the burly bovid, which I have only recently learnt is dying out due to rising temperatures in the Himalayan belt, is the sole source of all fresh dairy products, meats and winter attire.

It would be an absolute travesty if I did not mention the signature woollen yak cap worn by the locals in Tawang. Made of rough yak hair, it had six horn-like appendages made of the same wool, hanging out of its circumference, all pointing downwards. It might look odd to some, but I loved it. A cap I wished I'd been allowed to add to my unique cap collection. I did, in fact, try to get one in the local Tawang market at one of the little shops dotting the narrow winding roads, with the quaint black and brown winter caps hanging outside on display. I might have even got one, had I not offended 'Miss Tawang' – a lady in her sixties, somewhat of a local celebrity and owner of the largest shop in the area. The lady had won the beauty pageant in the area close to four decades ago. My expectations of meeting a beautiful Tawang woman dashed the moment I entered the shop and saw the old lady. My knack for putting my foot in my mouth was directly linked to not getting my hands on that cap. Mercifully, Miss Tawang didn't suffer from the narcissism and the laser eyes of the Homelander from the TV show The Boys (2019) *or I would have been toast.*

The inner chatter still on, I looked up at the sun, in the most beautiful of azure skies. Maybe, it had been around an hour since we had started climbing. Crossing a small stretch of meadow, we entered a dense part of the jungle and for the first time since we started out, I felt that the Jungle had insidiously started closing in on us from all sides, like it had taken us into its custody.

Shrubs were intertwined, making it impossible to move ahead. Trees were growing closer, their sharp and thin branches entangled. Thick canopies, towering trees slanting over. Wherever I looked, it was the same. A dense, almost impenetrable, network of vegetation surrounded us all around. We would have to cut our way out, one step at a time.

'Let's form a row,' Mike suggested as we entered the thicket. Using his stick, he started to clear the way but it didn't help. The sharp brambles would sway right back in his face, threatening to gouge his eyes out. 'Let's clear it with our hands,' I added, moving ahead of him and thrusting my hands slowly into the shrubs to make our way out. Certainly more helpful than the sticks but the hand-machete idea didn't come without peril.

A sharp branch pierced right through my shirt and as I pulled away, it tore my sleeve on its way out. Feeling my skin burn, I noticed little beads of blood pop up on my upper arm. Bruises and gashes didn't bother me, but jungle injuries weren't the same. Jungles, the hubs of all sorts of poisons, did not take to human intrusions kindly. Jungles fought back.

Mike, who was right behind me, quickly pulled out the first-aid kid from the ziplock bag and dabbed my gash with a medicinal gauze dipped in Dettol, which made it sting even more.

'Does it hurt too much?' Mike asked tenderly. I looked up bravely and chirped, 'Not more than my math results.' The examination results, which had been declared just as we left for Tawang, had been more painful than the injury. He looked up at me mischievously and asked, 'Did you make it?' I replied, sniggering cheekily, 'By a few marks.' Mike ripped open a Band-Aid but looked at the abrasion and put it back. Putting an inch-long Band-Aid on a four-inch gash was pointless. This would not be the only injury I was going to sustain that day ...

I had a long history of sport-related injuries. Innumerable trysts with gashes, abrasions and more. Growing up on stations where my father's fellow officers only had boys as children, I grew up as one of them. Like Mowgli from Kipling's The Jungle Book, *I was climbing trees, falling off them, cycling, playing football, wrestling in the mud, fist fights and getting hit in the face. My chin, knees and elbows bore testament to those daily injuries. To discourage me from my frequent adventures, the regiment's medical officer had time and again threatened me with daily tetanus shots. The adventures didn't stop, so I simply stopped reporting them.* This was me when I entered the Jungle that day.

When we came out on the other side of that crazy day, I didn't complain or cry. I fell into a deep silence. I knew the day would be indelibly imprinted in my memories. I felt lucky to be alive, but I held it all inside, only putting pen to paper when I was ready to face and share the lessons the day had taught me. There were many coming ...

P.S. Just because you don't complain, does not mean punishments won't come your way. It only means no one will know you are in pain.

25

'I'M HUNGRY!' GIGI WHINED.

We'd been climbing for over an hour, so I was half-expecting and dreading this moment. 'We reach there and then we eat, Gigi,' Mona said, pointing to an indistinct mountaintop as she led Gigi forward. Mona and I locked eyes, knowing there was no food to be had. I felt sorry. I shot a look at Neha but even if she was hungry, she did not let on. True to her nature, my sibling did not complain.

Many years ago, while my father was posted in Pattan, we would forage for food in Kashmir's apple orchards. But it was all a game. No quest of any sort was propelling us. Except fun and some juicy green apples.

While being herded like baby sheep and cattle to the only Army school in Srinagar, locked inside a three-tonne combat truck that had been custom-modified with a cage-like door at the back, we took turns to ensure the vehicle stopped while crossing the section of the highway dotted with apple orchards. One of the brats would throw a bag out, then a tiffin box and we would create a ruckus to distract the driver. Once the hapless fellow would stop and open the doors, like prisoners who hadn't seen sun in decades, the cacophonous mischief-makers would race towards the orchards. Neha, however, would continue to sit inside, not wanting to cause a nuisance. I, on the other hand, was part of the mischief-making pack and this game kept us busy during the nearly two-hour door-to-door sojourn to school.

If this were Kashmir, where we ran amok and incurred the wrath of the orchard owners, where juicy apple trees dotted the entire terrain, we would have had hope. But here, there was nothing we could eat. Thinking about the condensed milk we had lost, I cursed the waters. Salivating, I continued climbing, imagining everything I would eat when we got back. For a moment, the possibility of us not surviving the Jungle loomed over me, despite the promise I had made to myself.

Feeling terribly sorry for all the food we had lost, I turned to Gigi and Neha and said brightly, 'There is food waiting for us at the top, so hurry, girls.' Rohit looked at me silently. We both knew food was not on the cards anytime soon, but we had to keep the young ones from collapsing. I so wished that I had kept a few packets of chocolates in my pocket. The plastic wrapping would have kept them dry, even if they had got squished. Chocolates were not a luxury item, they were gritty field rations that would have been more advantageous than the hunter knife in my boot. None of us knew how to hunt in the wild.

'I've no ammunition. What use are cartridges in battle? I always carry chocolate instead.' The famed Captain Bluntschli had said in George Bernard Shaw's play *Arms and the Man*. The officer focused on the ability to survive, knowing fully well starvation is an undeniable possibility during war.

Alas! Wisdom in hindsight is a smug beast. It knows better but what is the point of knowing better after the pieces have fallen apart?

Barring Gigi and Neha, who had only had a sandwich each, the rest of us had not eaten since the morning and if Gigi hadn't brought it up, it would have escaped my attention entirely. My will to get us all home far outweighed anything else. It did not matter if I didn't get the new geared bicycle as my birthday gift or if I didn't make it to the junior basketball team! All I wanted was for all of us to come out alive. And especially the little ones, Gigi and Neha, had to survive.

As I cleared the path ahead and moved forward, my foot slipped and I slid down a slushy pathway to hit the bottom, face down.

Raising my head out of the mud, I laughed. I guffawed because I had had an out-of-body experience and seen myself slide, tumble and land face down. Lying spreadeagle in the slush and reduced to a hapless, ludicrous sight. My right elbow was bleeding, but I felt nothing in that moment. I turned and motioned Mike and Rohit to stay right there. I would find my way up. 'We go that way,' I said, pointing to them whilst spitting out the mud that had found its way inside my mouth and nostrils.

The Jungle was laughing. I understood why and cackled louder, part amused, part enraged. *Oh, how the mighty had fallen.*

26

ROHIT: '*WHAT NOW?*'

We stood silently gawking at what lay ahead. Still covered in mud, I scanned the vistas from left to right. Except for Bhalu's growls and ruckus of the crickets, there was absolute silence.

Turning around, I looked down the side we had ascended. It would be impossible to retrace our steps. There were no breadcrumbs to make a trail. No landmarks or jungle trail. The sun blinded me momentarily as I looked up. It had crossed the precise overhead mark, so it was clearly past noon. I was acutely aware and actively reminding myself that by 1830 hours, the sun would set and, if we were still in the Jungle, it would all be over. Time was ticking and with no working watch, I couldn't tell. God forbid, if the weather packed up again, the Jungle would be plunged into darkness much before sunset.

My arms were aching. My shirt torn in two places, both arms bruised and throbbing with pain, the younglings were hungry and tired and we had reached the top of the mountain only to discover that we needed to scale another.

Except the one in front of us looked a lot higher than the one we'd scaled, clouds hanging around its top like diaphanous cotton candy.

Importantly, the Red Bridge was nowhere in sight.

Without uttering a word, I started to descend. It was clear we had no other recourse. We had to go where the terrain took us. The mountains here had a peculiar undulating feel. The lush foliage and gentle ascent almost made them less intimidating to six little humans trying to get home.

Never judge a book by its cover: another learning that has stayed since.

Bhalu, Gigi and Neha, the new ragtag team, had banded together, deeply engaged in chatter. The two of them were exchanging notes about their respective dogs waiting for them back home. Even Gigi did not bring the topic of food again. The three followed, oblivious to the setback we had just had.

Amidst the range of mountains, we could no longer tell the direction of the Red Bridge. Some distance away, we could see what looked like a windmill, almost on the horizon. And suddenly, there was hope.

P.S. Hope can be wonderful. It can be dangerous too.

27

AN INTERLUDE

THE VOICE OF WISDOM IN HINDSIGHT CAN SOUND SMUG, sneering, annoying.

Everyone should carry a survival supply bag. A compass, map, mirror, an emergency first-aid kit, whistle, flashlight, a fully charged cell phone (with emergency phone numbers), bright-coloured or fluorescent clothing to attract aerial rescuers, some energy bars. Take some photos of the route you have taken.

Small first-aid kit: check.

The end.

While clicking photographs, make sure to include pictures with your hand pointing in the direction to go when heading back home.

Even if we hadn't lost the camera to the rivulet, we did not know how to use it this way.

Always check the weather forecast, plus the time of the sunrise and sunset. This will help you gauge the expected temperature changes to ensure adequate time to set-up camp.

We were familiar with the weather, but not the terrain. And which camp? It was supposed to be a picnic, not a trek.

In the mountains, communities are located around water supplies. If you find a river or stream, follow the water downstream. At some point it will pass by a road or a road junction and eventually it will lead you to habitation.

Yeah, that went well …

DO NOT PANIC!

Okay, so far so good.

Stop, stay calm, stay put and make your plan.

The plan was made keeping the daylight in mind. So stopping and staying put was not an option.

Sit down, eat and drink something.

Could we not go there, please? *Thank you!*

But we were not expert hikers or adults who had planned this. We were kids who had started out for a picnic and ended up here, lost.

28

DESCENDING THE MOUNTAIN TURNED OUT TO BE AN UPHILL task. Sheathed in thick foliage, sunlight beamed through patches where the canopies were lower and dispersed.

In the darker parts, every sound was amplified, almost echoing through the Jungle. Like the intermittent rumble of thunder from above, as if the Gods were in a slugfest. It felt like we were now in the very heart of the Jungle. A sudden screech of a bird, a flicker of something moving overhead, leaves brushing against the skin, or tumbling from the interlocked branches above, the rustle on the forest floor, everything was making us jump.

'Are there ghosts in this forest, Tina didi?' I turned to look at Gigi, marvelling at the timing of her question. Children are very perceptive of the energy around them. She was holding Mona's hand and walking slowly, 'Ghosts hide in trees and they like to eat children,' she continued.

I smiled, 'Who fed you this rubbish, Gigi?'

It wasn't helping that Bhalu was barking incessantly and at nothing in particular. Unnerving, given our predicament. Neha and I were walking holding hands. I looked up at the trees to ascertain if we had any company of the feral kind. It was hard to spot anything in that dense network of branches and dark green leaves. Bhalu and Gigi were both distracting me with their version of bow-bow and blah-blah!

Something was not right. You feel this kind of thing in your bones. Darkness creeping insidiously, descending without warning.

'Mama told me a story about two children who were picked up by a ghost and taken to a forest,' Gigi added animatedly. To which Mona shot back, 'It's not a ghost, Gigi, it's the witch in 'Hansel and Gretel'. And there are no ghosts in this jungle.'

Meanwhile, Mike, Rohit and I were trying hard to keep our eyes peeled on the way ahead, avoiding any trivial conversations. There was something eerie about this part of the Jungle. The roots were gnarled and criss-crossed, old and new grass jostling for space, ancient-looking moss over stones of all shapes and sizes – that had no allegiance to the grounds they were on and the uneven slope – it wasn't hard to tumble and roll down, gathering a lot of wet moss and more!

'Is there a witch in this forest, Didi?' Gigi asked conspiratorially. 'Will she put us in the big pot and eat us?'

'Shhhh, Gigi,' Mona said skittishly. Gigi's fearful questions were scaring her and the ominous surroundings certainly were not helping.

'You're a strong girl, Gigi, no witch can eat you,' Neha said, smiling. 'And there are no ghosts,' she added. My younger sister had never known the fear of the supernatural kind.

I sighed but said nothing. My inner voice rose …

I am the witch, Gigi. I put you in this bloody pot and made this mess of a stew. Don't you see it? The Jungle certainly does!

Mona regained her composure and shook her head, 'No, Gigi, no ghosts, no witches. Only us, okay? Don't worry and shhhh.' Mona and I exchanged looks. She seemed to have sorted the matter.

'But why is Bhalu barking?' Gigi insisted, her voice rising.

'Shhhhh,' Mona cooed. 'Bhalu is a dog. Dogs bark, Gigi, quiet now!'

Gigi had my attention at this; she had been warning us along with our furry companion, who had been duly barking beside us all along. But there was no time to speculate or be fearful. Quickening my pace, I added softly, 'Let's move a little faster before it starts to rain again.'

With my hair standing on end, I cast a careful look around, surveying the area from left to right. The thick wild grass was wet like sponge and squirting water beneath our feet. The trees looked awash too, which meant it had rained in this part of the Jungle very recently. With a strong gust of wind, the large leaves overhead dumped all the rainwater they had been holding, mimicking a cloudburst albeit small, the sneaky fellows! They seem to have waited till we were right under them! Bham!

Thank you very much. I get it! You take orders from the Jungle.

And while we were collectively cursing the miscreants for soaking us, a blinding sliver of light ripped through the foliage with an ear-shattering cracking sound and fell on a tree.

It lit up like a Christmas tree on Halloween and exploded. The freakshow was immediately followed by a thunderous boom, terrifying enough for anyone's blood to curdle.

My heart jumped out of my chest and I instinctively covered my head. *God damn! Duh-duhn, duh-duhn.*

When I opened my eyes, I saw a shivering Gigi clinging to Mona and Neha right next to me, her ears cupped with her hands. We sat on our haunches, huddled together like bunnies during winter. Mike and Rohit had taken cover behind a moss-covered rock. My ears were buzzing.

In the meantime, our furry companion had abandoned us again. The strike from hell had been too much for him. We heard receding yelps and then nothing. Bhalu had probably found a hiding spot.

Oddly, a gust of warm air drifted towards us and I realized that the cool crispness was gone. The stricken tree was aflame in one section. Looking keenly, I noticed that thick smoke was swirling out from its branches. It was a sight that belonged in a supernatural film about a duel between a wicked jungle and turgid skies. The poor tree was collateral damage.

The lightning had wrecked my notion that the Jungle was safer. We were not safe anywhere. Not by the water, not in the Jungle. Nowhere.

We'd heard of a cloudburst over the region that had caused landslides, washing away entire sections of winding roads and flooding the area. Many soldiers had been tragically swept away at the time. Their camps and barracks decimated within minutes. If grown men with military training could not survive the wrath of nature, what chance could we have?

'Let's go,' I spoke with urgency, my voice tremulous. Gigi had started to bawl and was refusing to budge. 'I am hungry,' she sobbed and dug her heels in. 'Let's go, Gigi, or the lightning will strike here,' Mona pleaded, struggling to stay calm. I was rubbing my ears vigorously, fearing I had lost my hearing.

'Where is Bhalu?' Gigi asked between sobs. Thunder roared, as the sky lit up again. Gigi clung to Mona even tighter. I saw paralysing fear in her eyes again, which alarmed me no end. I had seen it before and it didn't exactly bode well for us.

There was no time to cajole and plead. So before she could react, I lifted Gigi up and hoisted her onto my back, 'Come, we will go find Bhalu.' With that, I started to walk hurriedly.

Gigi did not protest or whine, instead she held on to me. The water had bonded us. Maybe, she trusted me.

As we continued descending, I looked at the devastation unleashed by the lightning strike. The hapless tree was still throwing out smoke and creaking, the foliage surrounding it singed.

I learned later that an average lightning strike can bring 100 million volts, which is roughly 53,540 degrees Fahrenheit. An inferno from hell.

'Everyone okay?' I asked loudly to which Mike motioned to his ears. 'They're ringing.' Pointing to mine, I shook my head. Everyone else was in the same boat too. The shock waves generated by the lightning bolt explained the blood-curdling sound and the ensuing effect on our ears.

For six younglings, the day was slowing turning into a nightmare. I was trying not to overthink and focusing on the way ahead. My heart thumping, Gigi on my back, I lumbered on. For the first time I noticed that we were all huddled together and moving quietly. The chatter had died.

We had come within a whisker of being electrocuted by lightning. It was providence that we hadn't been burnt to a cinder. Imagine six humans reduced to charred stick figures, still standing when found. Dark yet funny. The tree might probably have survived, not us. We would have been barbecued.

The thunder had silenced us. The tree catching fire in front of my eyes is still the most surreal memories of that day. Macabre and beautiful.

Was the Jungle alive and connected to the consciousness of the universe? Was it provoking the universe to punish the intruders? Was the universe a double agent? Saving us whilst executing the Jungle's diktat?

This was our second brush with the grim reaper on the same day. The lightning strike had changed the rules of engagement with the Jungle. Nothing could be taken for granted. Decidedly nothing.

P.S. I have never come this close to a lightning strike ever since. Do I consider myself lucky to have survived it? Yes, unequivocally. But let it also be said that I consider myself luckier to have witnessed this absolute marvel of nature. This and what I believe is the absolute sound of the Apocalypse albeit man-made and military in nature. If your father is a gunner, there was a very good chance you got invited for quite a few artillery firing exercises, especially the ones held at night.

'A bullet may have a name on it, but an artillery shell is addressed to whomsoever it may concern' is how gunners cheekily spoke of the lethal capabilities of their guns and gunner families were formally invited to witness the end of the world, if you please!

Sitting a few hundred feet away from Soviet-made, truck-mounted multi-rocket launchers, you bore witness to hell being unleashed. The idea of multiple rockets dispatched into enemy territory in less than twenty seconds, giving them little time to run for cover was scary enough but watching a live training exercise was something else. The decimation of the other side was guaranteed.

Every time a rocket was launched, massive firepower sent the near-molten back-plate of the rocket spinning back with exactly the same thrust as the rocket tearing through the night. You would not want to be anywhere near either ends. Many officers' wives trembled in their chairs at the sight and sound of doom. I recalled with rare delight how an officer's wife, who had probably never been to a rocket-firing exercise before, nearly fell off her chair in fright when the first rocket burst out of the barrel with a blood-curdling sound. That was the true sound of the Apocalypse. I've never heard anything quite like that since.

While I had borne witness to the side that unleashed hell, until this fateful day, I knew nothing about the other side. The site of the drop, the sitting duck; where hell fell, proverbially. Perhaps this lightning strike was the site of the drop, only with less devastation.

Today, I knew. I had seen both sides. I had lucked out. Been there, seen that. Better still, escaped it.

'Tis true, Nature is the true law! Nature does nothing in vain! Nature ain't no botcher.

29

'...AND THE HORSE STARTED TO SUDDENLY CANTER AND I was screaming!' the piggybacking Gigi was being regaled by a story from three years ago. We had cleared the treacherous thicket and were crossing the valley between the two mountains with Gigi on my back and a storytelling session in full flow. The skies were clear again, the sun's rays dancing on the stream running across the centre of the valley. To imagine that a lightning strike had near annihilated us just a little while ago seemed unimaginable given the pleasant environs volte-face.

The schizophrenic Jungle, blowing hot and cold with absolute impunity and lack of empathy for us.

'What is a canter?' Gigi asked curiously. I smiled and tried explaining, 'It is when a horse has decided to gallop but hasn't started yet. It's like jogging, Gigi.'

'Then what happened?' she egged me on.

'Well, I was a beginner and when the horse started cantering, I started to slip off its back,' I continued. 'Then what happened?' Her curiosity was piqued. I was enjoying telling her the tale equally.

'So, as soon as the instructor whistled to the horse to stop, I lost my balance and fell off,' I chuckled at the memory.

We had stopped and I set Gigi down. *Oh boy, was she heavy!* Mike and Rohit quickly refilled the empty bottles from the sparkling stream. Gigi, her face tear-stained from the post-lightning strike bawling, looked at me with concern and asked, 'Did you get hurt, Tina didi?' Mona had meanwhile cupped streamwater in her palms to wash the grime off Gigi's face.

'No, the riding ring had a lot of mud in it but you know Neha here, she ...'

'No!' Neha said, interrupting firmly. She was still embarrassed that she had left the reins when she saw me slip off the horse and that she could not handle my tumble and fell too. It was supposed to be our secret but the entire brigade knew it and the account had travelled home faster than a horse with a firecracker up its tail. The chatter centred around the logic of my fall and none whatsoever of my sibling.

I looked at Neha and decided against narrating the more interesting part of the account to the others. I had seen her release the reins during my fall and long before I hit the dirt. It had been an out-of-body experience, watching my own fall with great amusement. But she did let go of the reins voluntarily, her panicked cry of 'Didi' reverberating in the dusty riding ring. In her version, my adorable younger sibling had done so as she got distracted.

I may not have shared this with Gigi then but I am sharing this now, Neha. You left the reins while watching me fall. You were six or seven. Us sisters, forever bonded in our rises and falls, crests and troughs, happiness and sorrow.

The strange thing about a happy memory is that it holds within itself the incredible power of melancholia of a wonderful time that has slipped away and belongs in another realm now. The sweet innocence of childhood is replaced by experience that reins us all in, sooner or later.

Gigi extended her arms, a doleful puppy-look in her eyes. Clearly having enjoyed the ride and now oblivious to Bhalu's disappearance, she wanted to piggyback on the next leg of the journey. 'Come, Gigi,' Mike said and picked her up, as she mildly protested. It was my back she wanted. *The little spider monkey!* But Mike knew of the bruises on my arms. He was giving me a breather, *my sweet summer romance!*

'Gigi, don't be a spoilt brat,' Mona said commandingly, 'Get off and walk!'

Gigi took one look at her sister's eyes and slid off Mike's back quietly. Mona spoke like she meant business, she knew our stakes well. Gigi had to stop playing the baby.

After a short break at the base of the mountain, we started to move again. Looking up at the giant looming ahead of us, I wondered when all this would end – the adventure that none of us had signed up for.

Whatever happens to us today, we have to save these little ones, reverberated in me on a loop.

The Jungle was relentless and continually plotting – baying for young blood.

30

EXCEPT FOR A FEW MOSS AND LICHEN-COVERED ROCKY boulders that we scrambled up on all fours, the ascent was gentle. The environs were green and picturesque with no trace of civilization anywhere you looked. I watched with wonder as clouds floated across the sky, moving amorphously and lyrically as if they were performing a ballet. Surreal! All we needed now were some fairies and elves and a pack of friendly trolls! These were the same fellows who had obliterated the sun and dispatched shard-like raindrops to drown us. For a few moments, I forgot what we'd been through so far and wished I had my father's camera. Then I remembered the burning tree and hurried along.

The Jungle was like a mirage. Going after your mind, playing tricks, not letting you leave once you entered it. Were the Eagles sneakily referring to this when they penned 'Hotel California'? '*Welcome to Hotel California, such a lovely place/ You can check out anytime you like/ But you can never leave.*'

Mike was leading us now. Followed closely and in file by Mona, Gigi, Neha, me and Rohit right at the end. The little ones protected in the middle, our eyes on them. The legend of Badluram was back. Gigi and Neha sang in chorus. The ascent began in full earnest as we zigzagged our way up the mountain.

Now as we are all told, there is a proper science on how to ascend and descend mountains. If you join a hiking trek these days as a beginner, the trekking expert will brief you at the start. He'll talk about body positions and movement during an ascent, about walking with a straight spine, about leaning forward and keeping your weight on your toes and how to stretch your legs until they are completely straight. He'll emphasize the dangers of overexerting your ankles and knees, teach you about pacing and breathing, finding a rhythm between your breathing and strides, walking at a conversation pace and, finally, gradient adjustment, which means adjusting your centre of gravity to the gradient you are on while trekking.

I have often silently scoffed at those instructions. *Brother, been there and done none of that! Still breathing.*

The advantages of undertaking adventures, even accidental ones very early in life go hand in hand with being an Army brat. By the time you hit your twenties, you have lived many lives. You have smelt gunpower, seen rockets unleash hell, ridden on choppers, fallen off horses, fired from antiquated rifles, climbed mountains, played combat sports, moved schools and towns every two years, lived near jungles and deserts, learnt more than one language and a lot more. You manage to have lived a really rich life and have a lot to be grateful for.

'Look, berries!' Gigi said and broke away to grab some off the shrubs. They were growing all around us. While Gigi plucked a couple, Rohit made a dash for her. Grabbing her hand, he tried to pry them out but Gigi clinched her fist tightly and gritted her teeth in angry protest. She was hungry.

'Don't, Gigi! Throw them now!' Mona threatened, her hand in the air ready to smack her. Gigi promptly opened her fist and released the squished berries, their juices smeared all over her palms.

'They are poisonous,' Rohit said quietly and washed Gigi's hand with the water he had in his bottle.

'How do you know?' Mona asked urgently while yanking Gigi away from the shrubs. 'I saw the picture on the big board in the recreation centre at the adventure camp. They are the same ones,' Rohit said in a low voice, not wanting anyone to panic.

Like the evil queen from Snow White, the Jungle was trying every trick in the book to trip wire us.

Mona hissed at her sister, 'If you touch anything again Gigi, I will leave you here and the witch can eat you, do you understand?' There was hushed silence. Gigi read her sister's steely eyes and fell in line. Like a puppy after peeing on its human's prized Persian carpet, she knew she had erred.

But Gigi's hunger stung me. It was my fault they we were hungry and lost. Perhaps I was unconsciously using self-flagellation to get us out alive.

'Are you hungry, Neha?' I asked softly. She shook her head. I felt a lump rise in my throat, knowing the truth that she would not say. Shaking the sentimentality and guilt off, I squeezed her hand and kept my eye on the ball.

We continued climbing; this mountain, compared to the previous one, had less trees. There were rock features, thickly interconnected shrubs and meadows with lush grass for as far as the eye could see. We were at an approximately thirty degree incline from the ground with a good view of where we were going.

'Look! The windmill,' jabbing the air with my finger, I exclaimed eagerly. It was right there, close to the top of the mountain. A windmill meant human habitation. It meant the adventure would be over as soon as we got there. All we needed was to get to it and that's that! We would be rescued and reach home, relatively unscathed. I was breathless with excitement.

'What's on your arm?' Mona said stepping away from me, horrified.

Looking down, I jumped out of my skin, screaming and shaking vigorously. Attached to my forearm was the slimy predatory worm – the local blood-sucking resident of Tawang's jungles, the leech. It wasn't alone. There were three more on my other arm too. A large, longer one had strategically attached itself near my elbow that had bled earlier. I had goosebumps all over. Flaying both my arms in the air to shake them off, I was yelping and running around in circles.

The tiny leech had managed what raging waters and the lightning strike could not. It unsettled me completely, revealing my squeamishness for the creepy crawlies. I wanted to get it off but the very thought of touching them made me squirm.

'Take them off, take them off, please,' I was hopping, as though a rodent had run up my pants. As they sucked away to glory, the leeches had destroyed my superhero-like facade.

Rohit and Mike looked at each other, unsure of what to do. 'Remove it,' I screeched. Holding my arm, Mike gingerly caught the slimy thing between his fingers and tugged hard.

But as soon as he yanked it off my arm, blood burst from the wound like a hosepipe had been pulled off a running tap. Mike repeated the same on the other arm but as soon as he flicked it off, the puncture site bled profusely, and a steady stream of blood ran down my arm.

Yeah, bleed me dry, you sadistic Jungle!

Neha, who witnessed the bloody carnage, suddenly collapsed in a heap. As Rohit and Mona rushed to support her, I got my act together. Neha could not take it, the blood running down my arm was too much for her and she blacked out. While Rohit gave her a sip of water from his bottle, Mike tried wiping the blood off my arm and dressing the wound. I looked down at my feet and saw the tiny predators trying to get in through my shoelaces. Shaking my foot hard, I tried to throw them off before they latched on. If only I had still had my hoodie, I rued. My bruised arms would have thanked me for it.

'I'm fine, see,' I said, as Neha got up weakly. Rohit handed me a cotton gauze to press down on the two adjacent wounds. The bleeding had not stopped but Neha didn't need to know that. My sibling did not have the stomach for anything remotely bloody and more so if the affected person was a loved one.

But from this day on, we jokingly started to call it our *rigga-mouse* moment. Air-headedness followed by animatedly collapsing into a heap on the floor, hands and feet pointing upwards, stiff like a mouse with rigor mortis. Maybe we had seen it in a Tom-and-Jerry cartoon. I do not remember the precise origin of our private joke, but it has stayed since.

I glanced at the only leech that was still enjoying its happy hours at my expense. It looked a little bigger than it did a little while ago. As Mike tried to pull it off, I held his hand, trying to warn him against upsetting a skittish member of the erstwhile picnic party. With the leech on, we started to climb again. The bloody parasite was enjoying fresh blood from a hot-blooded human.

When Neha zonked out at the sight of blood, I asked Mike to not remove the last leech from my arm. Turns out, it was the right decision. We learnt later that leeches fall off on their own after they have had their fill.

This one had its fill, expanding steadily till it could guzzle no more and fell off. The site of the puncture continued to bleed but nothing like the ones that had been forcibly removed. An amicable parting of ways was decidedly better! The skin around the ones that had been pulled out was starting to itch.

As it turns out, leeches have deadly bacteria in their stomachs and if you try to pull them off, they can regurgitate the bacteria-mixed blood and dump it into the wound, infecting it. My arm was infected and would bleed till the next day, but more on that later. Strangely, the sight of blood has never made me squeamish to this day.

As we moved further, over the course of the day, leeches continued to hitchhike on my bare arms, even the exposed part of my neck. Every time there was a bruise from walking through the thicket, or we passed through shrubs, the worms found the bare areas on my arms and bingo! After a while, I stopped paying attention knowing they would fall off when well fed.

The bloody freeloaders!

Luckily, Neha, Gigi and Mona were wearing full-sleeved shirts and hoodies but we were careful to check for leeches that could get in through socks and the waist near the belts. Mike, Rohit and I, however, weren't that lucky.

How did they attach themselves without my feeling anything? Why did I bleed even after they fell off? I got answers from the Regimental Medical Officer, later. These creatures inject an anaesthetic into your skin when they sink their teeth in, making their bites painless. *Masterly!* So you don't realize when they latch on, which explained why I had not felt anything when they punctured my arms.

The second part of the answer was more vile. These jungle 'vampires' inject an anticoagulant when they latch on, which prevents the blood from clotting and that is how they get their uninterrupted, unlimited supply till their blood-filled bellies are ready to burst! So if you removed a leech before that, the wound would bleed for several hours or even days before the anticoagulant left your system. That explained the steady loss of blood when Mike plucked them off my arm.

I cursed the slimy bloodsuckers. The choicest of curses that I knew at the time were hurled with zero regard for propriety but I could not stop marvelling at how meticulously the universe had designed this micro-jungle predator. Anaesthetic and anti-coagulant in a tiny slithering worm body. *Brilliant!*

The anaesthetic, although entirely self-serving, spares the victim the pain of the puncture, and had the leech been a bigger creature, its anticoagulant could cause its victim to bleed dry. A mashup of kindness and absolute cruelty within the same creature. A contradiction, a paradox, call it what you will.

So, in essence, like the mighty homo sapiens, the leech is capable of kindness and ruthlessness in equal measure. Perhaps, both traits are imperative for survival and the universe knows it. It has taken me years to comprehend this duality and forgive the blood-sucking worms. Even the Jungle. Sometimes, even people.

P.S. The Jungle was turning out to be quite the Shylock!

31

AS WE SCRAMBLED TO THE TOP, THE LEECHES LATCHED ON. Mike and I raced towards the windmill, breathless with anticipation. The tiny but discernible speck from across the mountain was now within reach. We had hit a homerun finally. The people running the windmill would point us in the right direction. We would be rescued from this mess.

Was the zigzag ascent easy? On our young bodies, perhaps, it was. Suitably acclimatized children probably don't suffer on the mountains like the adults lugging around a plethora of health issues. Our bodies had not yet ravaged by decades of wrong lifestyle choices. We had good pairs of lungs, good knees and cholesterol-free arteries. It was an advantage which worked in our favour that day. Also, ignorance is sometimes bliss. Had we anticipated that it would turn into an unending day from hell, we might have reconsidered. Ignorance and arrogance can sometimes save you.

But our hopes were blown to smithereens as we got closer.

The blades of the small windmill were rotting and broken. It was still moving because its engineering and the wind was breathing life into it, but our harbinger of hope was a ruin. Left to rot and decay at least decades ago. While I had seen a few water-powered mills in the lower areas, the design of this one looked unfamiliar.

Grunting under my breath, I flung my stick at the windmill and sank to the grass, unmindful of the leeches I might pick up. Why was this happening? Why were we being punished repeatedly? I looked at the clouds that had floated in and surrounded us, bringing the visibility down again. Nothing looked breathtaking in that moment anymore. I was livid, at myself, at the windmill, at the Gods. At everything and at nothing in particular.

Anger improves nothing but the arch of a cat's back ...

Yeah, okay, shut up, will you?

I sat there, looking up at the relic of a bygone era. Meanwhile, the others caught up. The six of us looked at the dilapidated structure in silence – stupefied by this big upset now!

I am sure everyone's internal dialogue was exactly the same, except Gigi's, perhaps?

What were we going to do now? We hadn't a clue of our location. We could not go back, we did not know what lay ahead. The Red Bridge was nowhere in sight and another mountain stared us in the face. We were lost, lost like Alice, mad like the Hatter.

I sat on the grass, holding my knees, staring blankly ahead, wishing some teleporting device could just get us all out, right that moment. The others were silent too, looking lost.

Neha broke the silence first, saying, 'Let's go!' She was pointing at whatever the clouds did not let us see. To carry on to the end. I suppose we had no other choice. Never was a cat or dog drowned, that could but see the shore. Right?

I sprang up, drawing strength from my younger sister's calm grit and sense of purpose. Sensing that I was floundering, she picked me up. Optimists may go to hell, but death alone can kill hope! And death hadn't found us yet, so we still had reason to hope!

Trudging past the windmill, I touched its broken facade as if comforting it, saying my goodbye. Could it feel the rot and decay on itself? Did the abandonment make it melancholic? Did it miss the cacophony of humans milling whatever they milled here? As the clouds wafted along, the windmill slowly vanished from sight.

My wistful thoughts interrupted: *Whatever happens to us today, we have to save these little ones.* Reverberating within. On a loop.

We walked on into the clouds, descending with extra caution. Hoping.

32

THIS WALK IN THE CLOUDS WAS THE STUFF DREAMS ARE made of – an elixir for sore eyes and souls. An experience such as this transcends time and seeps in your very being. Was this how humans move between one life and the next? If there is indeed a next? Gently vanishing from one, appearing in another? This feeling hooks you and draws you to the mountains and its jungles year on year. Often, it becomes a voice in your head, urging you to become one with them, whispering its sweet seductions, not letting you go back to the concrete jungles ever again. An unlimited supply of endorphins and dopamine guaranteed.

We were walking among clouds. Not mist, not fog. Clouds. These magical beings, that happily soaked in the colours of the molten sun or dark rain and give it their own unique spin, were now giving us company. They were great tricksters too! As we started a fresh descent, they floated along gently, caressing the trees and going wherever the winds took them. Some thin and wispy, some thick like marshmallows, the clouds magically swirled all around us,

Sometimes Snow White, often the evil Queen. These fellows played both parts, unapologetically.

Our descent was like walking down a zigzag staircase from heaven, following the path of least resistance, and given the ever-changing visibility, taking each step gingerly to ensure we landed safely.

Gigi, with her arms reaching into the air, was attempting to capture the passing clouds; her tiny fingers extending into the condensed mass of water droplets as they passed by leisurely. With renewed vigour, we continued finding firm footing on the damp jungle floor. Rohit was leading and I was at the tail end. Walking at the end of our small group allowed me a view of the path as also the time to reflect on our next steps.

Once we had left the windmill behind, I had stopped looking up at the sun to check for time. That kind of self-induced stress was not going to change things now. We had to look ahead and not let the obvious challenges overwhelm us. Determined to get us all out, I knew fully well that anything was within the realm of possibility today, anything could come at us and send us hurtling down, literally, too. Anything could be turned against us. The many perils of trespassing on uncharted territory.

'My legs are hurt,' Gigi whined. Mona gave Gigi a once over, knowing her little sibling was using her baby voice to get what she wanted. Mona didn't mind. Gigi was a baby, afterall.

'Promise me you won't eat my strawberry lip balm again,' she said mock seriously. Gigi nodded, breaking into a grin, 'I promise' and then stuck her arms out to piggyback. Mona bent and let her little sister climb on. Both were grinning.

The arrangement would last only till you got home, sister! Little Neha had eaten up most of our mother's lipsticks while hiding under the bed when she was younger than Gigi. The red and pink ones, especially. Being caught with a mouthful of red, looking like the proverbial clown. Despite my mother's multiple warnings, the cravings for a scary red mouth continued unabated. So your lip balm didn't stand a chance, Mona!

'We'll take turns,' I said quietly, knowing it was hard to carry little Gigi for long distances. Mona smiled back and asked with real concern: 'How is your wound?' I noticed the swellings and a couple of new leeches. Looking at her, I shrugged. It was what it was.

I watched with absolute marvel as clouds floated past the trees and shrubs, left to right, playing peek-a-boo. Nature in a time-lapse. Taking it all in, I followed the five, glancing back every now and then to scan the Jungle. For nothing and everything. It was surely watching. My hunter knife was back in my left hand.

'Where is Bhalu?' Gigi suddenly enquired. We had all forgotten about our furry friend. With matted mountain hair all over and a happy face framed by a mane of brown fur, Bhalu was the quintessential mountain dog. Affectionate yet independent. We were travellers or intruders; we would be gone soon, one way or another. Did Bhalu have that knowledge when he chose not to return? Was he trying to not get emotionally attached?

Or, was it because he knew the Jungle wanted our heads on a platter and he did not want to be collateral damage? Never underestimate the instinct of a dog.

'Bhalu went to his home, Gigi, just as we will go home in some time,' I said.

Yeah, right! My inner voice sniggered. The other voice in my head shot back, echoing the famous lines by Robert Frost. 'The woods are lovely, dark and deep, but I have promises to keep and miles to go before I sleep.'

So, help me, God!

Timing is everything, and like a lot of wise people have rightly said, for anything truly remarkable to happen to you, you have to be in the right place, at the right time, every time.

We heard it coming!

Had we been at the windmill under the open sky at this precise moment, or even in the raging water, this adventure would have ended faster. Had we been delayed perhaps by just thirty minutes, it would have put a lot of people out of misery, even those back home who probably knew by now that we were missing.

33

WE HEARD IT COMING. IT WAS AN UNMISTAKABLE SOUND. The sound of my father leaving base for his regular aerial reconnaissance of the region. We would often run out of the barracks in the morning and watch with awe as he and the Air Force pilot in grey-blue dungarees took off in their mean machine. The helipad was a few hundred metres from the residential barracks and in its direct line of sight.

Battling fickle weather, the single-engine Cheetahs were pressed into service to survey our borders with China as Tawang was right on the border.

Whup! Whup! Whup! We heard it coming. The Cheetah helicopter was furiously beating the air with its powerful blades and coming towards us.

The sound was getting closer by the second, the trees around us feeling the impact of its powerful rotor blades. We looked at each other, our hearts beating , pupils dilated, brimming with hope of an impending aerial rescue.

'Ayeeeeee yeeehhhh ayeeeeeee … we're hereeeeeee!' We welded our cries with all the desperation, excitement and fear. As the Cheetah got closer, and while we could not see it clearly,

we raised our hands in the air, waving wildly, screaming and jumping, uttering what would have sounded like gibberish. Surely the pilot's peripheral or oblique vision would notice us. Surely they were out looking for us.

'Herreeeee, ayeeeeee, down hereeee!'

The chopper was directly overhead, our hearts pounding like an anvil chorus, the trees around us swaying as a powerful gust of wind hit them like a hurricane, forcing them to dangerously sway side to side. It seemed to be flying low.

Our rescue had arrived. It was probably hovering right above and soon we would be thrown the swaying ladder and be fished up one by one. We would send Gigi and Neha up first and then they would fly another two sorties to get the rest of us out. I would go on the last one. My head was abuzz with how this disaster of a day would end. Once the helicopter took off with me on board, I'd be looking down on the Jungle, sticking my tongue out at it.

Then the Cheetah crossed us and flew past.

No! No! Nooooooooo!

Neha and I suddenly broke formation and rushed down the mountain as fast as was possible, chasing the sound of its whirring blades. Still screaming and flaying our arms wildly. The whirring receded as quickly as it had come upon us and the two of us stopped following it. You could not chase and catch a chopper's attention whilst running down an uneven slope. One task was hard enough. Besides, it was too late.

The feeling in the pit of the stomach on coming within a hair of triumph and then fail is excruciating. It is like a hard punch in the gut. You keel over on impact and not because of a hurting solar plexus alone. Your spirit, your will to go on, your resilience come is under fire. You are truly tested.

As we stood there panting, our faces flushed from the sudden sprint, the other four joined us quietly. There was silence, every sound of the jungle audible now, even its silence.

'The trees were too thick for …' Mike's voice trailed off. There was nothing to explain. He knew. We knew.

On this side of the mountain, we were under an impregnable tree cover. In jungle gear, not a single fluorescent item on us that could catch anyone's eyes. We were in the wrong place, under a thick jungle canopy, at the wrong time, yet again!

Timing is like a magic window. You have got to be around when it opens and rush at it. That window, given the odds, never did open for us.

It was a whole different matter that the Cheetah was not looking for us. It was on its routine reconnaissance, perhaps with my father on board, perhaps unaware of the fate of six brats from the base, including his two children. Or, maybe not.

What we did not know was that roughly around the same time, a small patrol party had just arrived at the site by the mountain where our truck had broken down. Word had gotten out that we were missing …

34

'WHAT IF THIS MOUNTAIN TAKES US STRAIGHT TO THE Chinese?' Mona said suddenly.

A half hour or so later, we were still on the mountains, climbing, scrambling, finding our way to the Red Bridge: the Godot in our lives. Apologies, Mr Beckett, but we seemed to be going nowhere, much like your Vladimir and Estragon, who had endless discussions and encounters whilst looking for Godot. And Godot never showed up.

'How is that even possible?' Rohit said quietly. 'We would have to reach the Indo–China border first and then cross over to the Chinese.'

'I mean what if we are in some sort of no-man's land right now?' Mona said with absolute seriousness.

Mona's words got me thinking. What if she was right? What if we were actually in no-man's land? The mountains were uninhabited. Except for the abandoned windmill, we had encountered nothing that remotely suggested there were human beings around. Lama Wangchuk, the local Tawang boy hand-picked to participate at our camp, had told us of how often Indian shepherds strayed over to the other side and Chinese ones landed up on our side with their yaks. Now, that was only possible if the borders were unfenced for hundreds of miles.

Lama Wangchuk was a good-looking, shy, guitar-strumming Tawang boy who participated in the adventure camp two years in a row. By the second year, Lama, aka Lemon, had opened up to us and a little note had found its way to my bunk. Lama had professed his affections. I liked him but the impracticality of our situation killed whatever chances there were. I'd go back and he'd stay right there. What then? Mountainfolk belong in the mountains. They must not descend, it's heartbreaking for a lot of them.

'If the China catch us, will they beat us?' Gigi spoke suddenly.

'The Chinese, not the China,' Mona said laughing. 'No, they will not beat us, Gigi.' Neha and Mike were chuckling too.

My Lama Wangchuk-induced reverie was broken. What if we were found by the Chinese?

Could we be called prisoners of war and put in jail?

No, duh, only soldiers are called prisoners of war!

But what if they blackmailed our fathers and wanted money to get us back?

Since when did soldiers earn that sort of money? But the Army would get us back. We are only children.

Wait till they find your hunter knife and hear your insolent voice!

Bull! They'll just send us back as a goodwill gesture. Hindi-Chini bhai-behen!

The voices in my head were having a field day.

Mona's concern and my inner dialogue had fired up the possibility of being actually found by the other side. If they were to 'nab' us, I imagined all of us being packed off to some Chinese sweatshop, where we would end up assembling cheap smartphones or cheaper Diwali lights for the Indian markets. Ah, well! Minor mercies, this happened some moons ago.

The clouds passed and the sun shone again, its golden hue cutting through the foliage in vertical shafts, creating pools of warm light in our line of sight. The warmth and light brought hope. Whatever it took, one way or another, we were going to go home.

'I almost failed in mathematics,' I blurted to divert everyone's attention and chuckled. The young ones sniggered. 'And my mother was furious'.

'It's okay, I failed in social science exam, T,' Gigi chirped.

'Tina didi, Gigi,' Mona corrected her.

'And I wrote *dhobi kapde seeta hai* in my Hindi exam,' Neha chuckled at her own anecdote.

Neha's response in her examination on the occupation of a washerman had been a matter of great amusement for us all. According to her, the washerman stitched clothes. Gigi giggled at Neha's blooper, to which my sister responded with a quick rejoinder, 'Tell us, Gigi, what are foods that give us good health called?' Gigi shot back without hesitation, 'Strawberry ice cream!' Her response evoked a collective chuckle.

Neha laughed hard and hugged her, 'That is why you failed, Gigi!' and then added, 'my mother makes the best strawberry ice cream, I will ask her to make some for you.' Our mother's ice-cream recipe was truly special.

I smiled and then instantly fell silent.

My thoughts went to my mother. She would be worried sick. Did my father know? I was thinking about them right now. While my father would calmly but swiftly do what was needed to be done, I knew that my mother was a whole other ball game. I felt sorry for what I had put her through. She was raising us singlehandedly while Dad slogged at the borders. She absolutely did not deserve to lose both her kids like this. That, too, during a vacation!

Most people cannot fathom how hard the life of an Army wife can be. It involves long periods of separation from their husbands often, bringing up children alone, filling in for the fathers and perpetually living with the lingering fear that the husband might come home in a coffin. I had seen my mother struggle ever since my father left for the borders a few years ago – and I was old enough to register it. Also, it didn't help that I was inching towards the terrible teens at the time. I was a handful, to say the least.

Sorry, Mom!

I snapped out immediately; there was no room for sentimentality. The chopper was gone but we had to keep going, wherever the mountains took us. They were taking us somewhere, for sure.

'Gigi, tell me what is that?' Neha said pointing to a purple flower. All around us, was a meadow-like stretch filled with flowers that had a rich purple hue. 'Wow,' Gigi exclaimed with wonder. Orchids growing in the wild is not a common sight but here there were! If Kashmir had tulips, Arunachal had orchids. In fact, over fifty per cent of India's orchid species are found in Arunachal Pradesh alone and, hence, the moniker 'Orchid State'. Of all my father postings, I remember Pattan and Tawang with the most fondness. Although, Tawang had an edge over Kashmir's Pattan, as I was older now. Strong memories, more awareness, perhaps more agency. Old enough to know ... and yet, not old enough to know better, if that make any sense.

The purple-hued flowers were everywhere, sprouting from cracks within rocks and growing at whatever angle the undulating mountains allowed them. This wasn't some sort of resistance. They loved the mountains, their 'motherland', so to speak.

Gigi's eyes beamed with curious delight as she inspected the purple orchids in her hand. Having plucked a few on the way, she was lost in a childlike reverie. Perhaps, some inner monologue about God's great creation or simply put, fascinated by the distinct purple colour she'd not seen before.

Regrettably, I did not have the luxury to soak in the beauty of the place. I had to get us home, in one piece.

I don't recall how long we had been walking when I

heard bells. They clearly sounded like the bells around the necks of domesticated animals. The sounds were coming from somewhere above, which meant that somewhere up ahead, there was human habitation or a shepherd.

Energized, we quickened our pace. I pushed through a cluster of shrubs that cut my right arm just below the elbow. Again. The adrenaline rush had resurfaced. I didn't feel the pain. Pressing down on the cut, I urged everyone to walk faster towards the sounds.

35

'A CHICKEN SANDWICH AND TANG, TINA!' GIGI EXCLAIMED happily.

'It's Tina didi,' Mona interrupted crossly.

'It's all right. Tina is not disrespectful,' I replied chirpily. *For the first five years of my life, I had addressed my father by his pet name. Unlike my disapproving mother, my father did not mind it at all; in fact, he loved it. It was not disrespectful, he would tell my mom. Although, I think he was terribly amused by it.*

We were excited at the prospect of being found and Gigi was imagining the food she would savour when we found the yaks and its shepherds.

The ascent was steep again so our walking sticks were being put to good use. Loose moss-covered rocks paved the way as we scrambled up. We had to be careful lest we slipped and tumbled, facing other Jungle horrors on our way down.

Gigi was walking alongside Mike, Neha walking right behind him. The two chattered as the six of us trudged on.

'And what if they don't have chicken sandwiches, Gigi, will egg mayonnaise do?' Neha added, salivating. Her favourite sandwich comprised a filling of mayo slathered on finely chopped pieces of boiled egg, and we had carried a few today. *Alas!* Gigi considered the option and responded happily, 'Then I eat mayomase sandwich.'

'It's mayo-nnaise, Gigi,' I said, as Mona chuckled. Like most six-year-olds, Gigi tripped on complicated words, invoking gasps of adoration from the girls.

I looked at Mike and smiled. Like the rest, I too was hopeful but Mike said nothing. We had had enough setbacks today and he was not one to jump to any sort of conclusions. We were a good pair in the making, I thought, the two of us. My teenage impishness was offset by his calm, collected and dependable demeanour.

'I could eat a horse,' Rohit said quietly as we negotiated another rock feature. 'And the math wizard finally speaks,' I said, laughing.

Mike joined in teasing, 'How about we make that a yak, bro?' Rohit smiled and shot back. 'Okay, I could live with that.'

The banter had drawn in the quietest among us, a very welcome change. After all, nobody had heard Rohit express himself so openly, not today at least. The morale of the group was high, having collectively put aside all our previous setbacks, we were following the distant sound of the bells. Hopeful like the metaphor of the soaring eagle.

The weather was playing along too. Clouds drifting merrily across the azure skies and a happy cacophony of birds adding to the atmospherics. Despite the bruises and leeches, for a few moments, it felt like the picnic we had set out for that morning. With a happy ending.

36

'CAN'T HEAR THE BELLS,' MONA SAID, WITH RISING ALARM. We were near the top now and for as far as the eye could see, it was just the jungle and highlands. And zero yaks.

Had we been imagining the sounds of those bells? Was this a mirage, our mountain version of it? Silence fell upon us as we scanned the terrain for any sort of movement. Yaks moved slowly, so those bells would give them away. But, there was nothing to find. No yaks and no shepherds.

We were back to square one.

'The air is clear in the mountains so those sounds could be coming from much further,' I said, thinking aloud, still trying to keep my own hopes up. It could probably be true. We clearly had not been hallucinating so the yaks were perhaps somewhere out there, being tended to by men who could help put us on the road back home.

'Let's keep walking,' Mike said quietly and we did. The path ahead was another stretch of Jungle and highland, which would lead us somewhere for sure. And before dusk, if we were lucky. As per my calculation, it was probably around 1400 hours at the time. Maybe a bit more. We would know soon enough.

37

Badluram ka badan zamin ke nichey hain, Badluram ka badan zamin ke nichey hain,
Badluram ka badan zamin ke nichey hain, toh humein uska ration milta hain …
Sabashh … hallelujah …sabashh …hallelujah

SABASHH HALLELUJAH, TOH HUMEIN USKA RATION MILTA HAIN! The legend of Badluram reverberated in the highlands as we sang in unison again. Maybe there was a Rifleman Badluram waiting for us, maybe he would show us the way, maybe we would partake of some of those rations that the regiment sang about, maybe he would rescue us. Who knew! But we sang because it kept us buoyant. There were legends of many soldiers who protected their own, many from beyond the grave as well. Badluram's legend was only the most energetically lyrical.

Truth be told, we were not singing to be saved, we were singing to survive. Not for a moment had I forgotten the promise I had made to myself right after crawling out of those waters. *Whatever happens* … I continued moving forward, thinking only about what lay right ahead of us. Giving up was not an option.

Another dense highland, an endless trek, with Badluram for company. I was holding Neha's hand and walking alongside. It was my way of telling her that we would survive and I would not let anything happen to her. To little Gigi too. Neha and Gigi sang throatily, swinging their hands together to the beat of the song. We all sang together.

Singing, the things it can do! Lift your spirits and put a song back in your step. Put you back in the saddle, so to speak! It can shift your energy, shoo away your worries and make the path ahead seem bearable and almost pleasurable. We looked up and saw another mountain we had to climb.

This ascent was like all the previous ascents. We walked in file for the most part, keeping an eye ahead and one at the back. Our singing was punctuated by periods of silence and, during those silent stretches, while we were navigating the terrain, the Jungle spoke and sang and whispered. It was an impromptu concerto of chirping, humming, thrumming and buzzing. Crickets chirping at what sounded like a hundred decibels, birds calling out to each other announcing our arrival, leaves rustling everytime the wind caressed them; all working in harmonious tandem to remind us that the Jungle was alive and watching us.

'Why do insects make so much noise?' Gigi asked innocently, as we continued climbing. She was referring to the crickets and it was certainly a burning question for us brats.

We had heard them chirping our entire lives. Army establishments and cantonments were built on the outskirts of cities or in remote locations, sometimes near forested areas. Within those cantonments, countless flora and fauna breathed and cohabitated with humans. Crickets, snakes, scorpions, insects, frogs, giant chameleons, and all kinds of spiders. Often peacocks, deer and sambars too. Peacocks dancing and prancing in your garden and cobras slithering into bathrooms were common sights. At evening get-togethers, officers would often joke about staring down a cobra from the hotseat in the bathroom as they continued reading the newspapers nonchalantly and how the perhaps bored reptile had slithered away through the drainpipes. And these stories were true. Cantonments perennially throbbed with life and the sound of a gazillion crickets throughout the day, but you could hear them reverberating more clearly at night.

Male crickets produced these chirping sounds by rubbing their leathery front wings together to attract female crickets as mates through a process called 'stridulation'. *The things that the female of a species can fall for, sometimes beats me!*

'The crickets are singing loudly, Gigi, not making a noise,' Neha said smiling. The most mellifluous amongst the six had spoken. She had tuned in as we were trudging on and she believed they were singing. Well, they were 'singing' to their ladies alright! *Ironically, Neha didn't take to singing professionally. A travesty really, given the kind of voice the gods had bestowed upon her. She became a banker instead.*

It was true that we were up against an intimidating adversary but it was also true that our deepest roots as humans were truly with nature. Was that why the Jungle hadn't finished off the little humans yet? Was someone or something looking out for us?

'Tina!' Mona shouted excitedly, bringing my distracted ruminations to an abrupt end. Being the tallest, Mona had seen ahead before the rest of us and as we climbed a few more metres, we could see it too.

We had arrived at what looked like a small village. Built on the mountain incline, a line of old wooden huts and two barn-like structures stared us in the face. I gasped in disbelief. Habitation had found us when we had least expected it.

38

FOR THE BETTER PART OF THE DAY, THERE HAD BEEN NO headway, respite or food. It had been an endless trail and the Jungle had not exactly handled us with kid gloves. For a band of lost children, the day had been harsh and unrelenting, so the village appearing in our path was really God-sent!

Conjured out of thin air! When we had least expected any sort of miracle, there it was. Some fifty-odd metres ahead of us. Leaving us stumped and dumbfounded. For a moment, we didn't know what to do. Then almost instinctively, we huddled together. Like rugby players before the start of the game, only we were babbling over each other's voices.

Rohit: Let's ask them about the nearest road?

Me: They can at least point us to the river? Maybe we have been climbing parallel to it?

Mike: We should get some food first.

Mona: See that old woman there? Let's talk to her.

Me: Maybe they know of the nearest Army base?

Neha: Will they … er … have a phone here?

Gigi: We eat Mayomase sandwich?

Gigi cooed and settled the matter. Food in the belly first. Whatever the villagers offered would be welcome at this point. Yak meat, even milk or vegetable stew. Our mouths salivated at the possibilities.

In the Army, it's often said that when you set out on your missions, you have got to have one meal in your stomach and one packed for the road as you'd never know when you would get your next break or meal and a soldier must never operate on an empty stomach! Planning for contingencies is considered crucial for survival.

With food on our minds, we quickened our pace and hurried towards the huts. I was a bit overwhelmed and perhaps a little relieved too. The day was finally going to end well and lift a mammoth load off my guilty back.

I reckoned they would escort us to the nearest exit point or point us towards the Red Bridge. Maybe they would even escort us all the way to the base, and, most definitely, we would get something to eat. Whichever way you looked, we were safe now and no longer at the mercy of the Jungle.

As we got closer to the settlement, a couple of men walked out of the wooden huts and spotted us. Their faces, like most people in the Northeast, were ruddy and freckled (more red blood cells to compensate for lesser oxygen at these heights), also wrinkled by the harsh light of the mountain sun. It was hard to guess their ages but they looked in their thirties. As we got closer, we noticed that the men were staring at us.

There were women sitting outside, knitting wool. Yak wool, I suppose. One of them was putting small pieces of yak meat out to dry. In the region, they chewed on dried meat to keep them warm during the harsh winters. The locals would painstakingly cut and dry yak meat all summer so come winter, when avalanches blocked roads and fresh food trucks got stuck, yak meat kept them warm and healthy.

The women looked really old, with deep crevasse-like wrinkles on their faces. They reminded me of Miss Tawang so I shook my head, attempting to get rid of the ill-timed thought. Looking at Mike and Rohit, I was wondering how to break the ice when three more men emerged from the barn-like structures. One of them looked younger than the rest. He was also the tallest among them, unusually tall for the region.

We continued walking in their direction, waiting for a smile or a gesture, just about anything to help us strike a conversation. There was none. As we got closer, we were able to see them clearly. Their faces were deadpan but their eyes were a dead giveaway.

They did not look happy to see us. In fact, the very opposite. We were intruders and clearly not welcome in their village.

But how could this be? It did not seem to make any sense and frankly stunned me a wee bit.

I observed how they stood their ground and watched us get closer. Goosebumps on my leech-ravaged arms, my instinct was ringing alarm bells in my befuddled head.

The hostility was so palpable that Gigi, who was walking alongside, grabbed my hand and tightly squeezed it. Even the youngest among us had picked up on the tension brewing in the air. I shot a glance at Mike and knew he was thinking the exact same thing. We had to get out of there fast. In all that nerve-wracking tension, Neha and Mona were walking right behind me silently, and likely wanting to run.

The men neither moved, nor uttered a word but they followed us with their razor-sharp eyes until we had crossed them. Like in an old western, we felt like the intruders on horsebacks who were looked upon with deep suspicion by inhabitants of the remote township! But we were not bandits. We were just children who were lost. Surely they could have sensed that?

'Road on which side?' Rohit managed to blurt out to the men. 'Road,' he motioned with his hand again. Alarmed, I warned him, 'Don't.' The men looked on crossly and then started to speak amongst themselves, flaying their arms as they spoke. Their body language was visibly aggressive. There was an urgency in their tone and since we could not decipher a single word, it sounded even more intimidating.

This tryst with fellow human beings was supposed to be our miracle, but even in our wildest imagination, it wouldn't have ended in a massive anti-climax. And yet …

In hindsight, if Lama Wangchuk were with us, this could have gone differently. He spoke the local languages, Hindi and English, too, and could have communicated better with the villagers, ending our ordeal quickly. But then again, if Lama had been with us that day, this picnic would never have become the adventure that it did. He knew the terrain and the Jungle. The Jungle knew him too. It would have spared us and this day would have amounted to nothing.

'Keep moving,' I whispered urgently, while thinking of the knife tucked in my boot. It would take me a few seconds to pull it out and brandish it.

My mind racing, I was thinking of a course of action to defend ourselves.

We had all taken judo classes at the adventure camp, so those would come in handy! Neha and I were learning karate back in school and had advanced belts. Neha, a blue belt already and an inter-school silver medallist, could surely lead the charge. Mike and Rohit would do fine in a hand-to-hand combat. And all of us would protect Gigi. Followed by Mona, only because she reeked of fear. Earlier that year, I had kicked my black-belt instructor in the private parts and brought him down during a training session, albeit inadvertently. He was a tall man and my short-ish leg could not make it to his solar plexus. Now this particular kind of *un*-skill could be put to good use here, especially on the tallest amongst them, and just because my leg would only reach that far up! Like Lao Tsu said in *The Art of War*, 'Let your plans be dark and impenetrable as night, and when you move, fall like a thunderbolt!'

All in all, if things went south, our combined martial arts training might give us a fighting chance. After all, our adversaries would not expect any kind of fight or resistance from a group of young children. What chance did we have? To them, the odds would seem stacked against us. In my mind however, if push came to shove, if our survival depended on it, we would win.

Survival is such a powerful instinct. It displaces fear. It reveals our innermost core to us. In that one day, I learnt more about myself than I would have in an entire lifetime. Threadbare, down to the very bones. It is a whole different matter that it has taken me years to process it. Even to this day, when I enter a space, be it a theatre, an eatery, a nightclub, an office, even a nature or river trail, I first scan for exit points and trouble spots, just in case. My subconscious reflexes starting to think of the fastest way out. So if the dots were ever to be connected, it would all come back to this day in the jungle.

Back at the village, without wasting a minute or uttering another word, we hurried past what looked like an empty animal enclosure. We kept moving. The village was behind us now but one could still hear voices.

It was the third most disquieting moment for me during that day and by far the most disappointing. The Jungle had tested us through out the day but I had no grand expectations of kindness or of mercy from it. Those illusions had long been shattered. We would have had to fight our way out. But as a child, I just could not fathom why the village folk had been antagonistic towards us.

Was Mona right? Was this village in no-man's land and hence the grand reception? Or, had we crossed into Chinese territory or China-annexed Arunachal Pradesh and hence the hostility? In these regions, while you could not tell a Tawang local from a Chinese, the six of us looked discernibly different. We stuck out like sore thumbs. Although a majority of the young locals understood Hindi and spoke in it decently, curiously the villagers we had encountered spoke a language we did not understand. Was it Mandarin? Some of the locals also believed they were Chinese. Oftentimes, people living along borders are known to feel conflicted about their identities. Or, maybe they were deeply private folks who just did not like the intrusion. Since we were wearing camouflage pants and jungle boots, did they assume we had military backgrounds? Should that not have helped? Should we have tried to appeal to the women? Should we have in the least requested food for Gigi and Neha?

Again, this was all wisdom in hindsight, an analysis by paralysis! At the time, we did what we deemed safe, to scram as fast as we could.

All that notwithstanding, a small 'adventure junkie' part inside me still believes we had crossed into Chinese-occupied territory that day. But of course, I will never know for sure.

39

THE STAKES WERE HIGH IF WE HAD ACTUALLY CROSSED over. International borders were perpetual flashpoints and tinderboxes and a single event could snowball into a full-scale conflict.

Recently, amidst the Indo–China faceoff triggered by the Galwan Valley 'skirmish', reports circulated of the alleged abduction of a P. Ringling and four others by PLA personnel from Sera-7 on the international border. The five were working as porters for the Indian Army along the LAC in Arunachal Pradesh. Ringling, a student, had returned home due to the COVID-19 restrictions and taken up the job of an Army porter for sustenance. While the news erupted and social media slammed China for its high-handedness, the Chinese government announced a few days later that the five had been found on their side and would be handed back. And they eventually did. But it was clear that everything that happened along the borders had the chance of snowballing into an international incident.

We were lost somewhere along those very volatile and sensitive borders and the day was nowhere near its end.

Looking back, had our adventure taken place now, the hullabaloo an incident like this could have created nationally was inconceivable. The media would have reported that the six of us had disappeared on the Army's watch and surfaced on the Chinese side. Social media would have plastered our pictures up and tagged the world at large. And we could have been traded to their absolute advantage. Now, maybe I had overthought it and we would have simply been 'handed back' as a goodwill gesture, but all of this could have happened. You could blame my state of mind for it, given the day we were having. Nothing was beyond the realm of possibility.

Thankfully, this misadventure happened when times were simpler, village folk were just village folk – life existed beyond the internet and everything didn't get blown to smithereens on social media.

And while an international incident might have been momentarily avoided, a strange kind of fatigue was starting to set in. I was feeling emotionally drained.

Leading everyone out of the jungles was turning out to be harder than I had expected and the ensuing responsibility felt like a crown of thorns. Had I bitten off more than I could chew? It most certainly felt like that. Did everyone else need to be punished for it? Absolutely not. R. Scott Bakker's words in the *Judging Eye* crossed my mind, 'Too often, the measure of power lies not in the number who obey your will, but in the number who suffer your stupidity.' In my case, it was both.

With mild regret and a truckload of self-belittlement (at the time, I did not know what it meant), I lumbered on and, for the first time that day, I secretly conceded that we were lost. I was lost. The Jungle had managed to turn fellow humans against us so there was a good chance it was going to have its way today …

40

'ALL THIS IS HAPPENING BECAUSE OF CHARLIE,' I MUTTERED under my breath. Mike and I were climbing together, a little ahead of the rest. 'No,' he responded, chuckling with a naughty glint in his eyes, 'although what you did to him was quite something!'

'Well, he kind of deserved it and … maybe I deserve this,' I said, my voice tapering pensively.

'Relax, it was a prank,' Mike said squeezing my hand. I smiled back but Charlie was on my mind.

As it goes, Charlie wasn't his real name. But because of what I had done to him, he had been rechristened. AC, as we called him, had come in strutting on the first day of the adventure camp. His swagger and smugness were annoying, as were his misogynistic comments to all the boys in the camp, 'Don't be a pansy like a girl.' In his mind, being a girl equalled being a coward. AC was his school's cricket captain – apparently a good one – but he was also a bully with a grandiose illusion about his machismo.

Might I add, the fellow was hairy like a gorilla, his legs barely visible from beneath the dense foliage. 'Real men have hair!' he would say proudly. 'Sharma, shave or wax or whatever, you're a girl, right?' At the time, I hadn't got the ball rolling on the excruciatingly painful hair-removal rituals yet. AC enjoyed his insults much like soldiers enjoy their Patiala pegs of Old Monk. And I was not the only one at the receiving end. By the time the camp came to an end, he had name-called and bullied everyone. Consequentially, the campers were fed up and something needed to be done. And it was.

Two days before the camp ended, I had procured a tube of hair-removal cream from the small canteen counter at the camp. So in the dead of the night, while he snoozed like a bear in deep hibernation, Mike, along with a fellow dorm mate, slathered the hair removal cream on his gorilla-like legs and some on his dangling left arm.

The next morning the sounds of a shrill 'Oh shit, oh shit' echoed in the boys shower room and all the way to the girls dormitory. AC squealed 'like a girl' and I became a bit of a hero at the camp. With the jungle of hair gone from both his legs and left arm, he resembled a plucked chicken, and as he slinked past the 'hall of shame' for breakfast, we stood at the door of our dormitory cackling like hyenas. Justice had been delivered. And that is how AC became a Charlie!

'You'll pay,' he had said, gritting his teeth after he discovered who the mastermind was.

I had heard about good and bad karma often from the elders in the family, so Charlie and the concept of divine justice were playing in my mind. It was a prank and, sure, he deserved it but clearly every action had a consequence.

Who knew it better than me right now? Also, he was not the only one I had pranked at the camp that summer. See, we had a snitch in our midst …

Our snitch's claim to fame were her cascading knee-length golden brown hair that she combed and cleaned and preened over for hours at end as we all watched in awe. But we soon became aware that Rapunzel had started to tell on us for our midnight raids at the Mess hall and kitchen. At the camp, the rules were sacrosanct. Dinner at 2000 hours and lights out at 2030 every night. Curfew was imposed thereafter till 0400 hours on the next morning. But what kind of a brat retired to bed at 8.30 p.m.? Raiding the kitchen for pineapple cans, baked beans and chocolate éclair toffees was deemed our right, considering the adventure-filled daily schedule. Our raiding party of four sneaked out of the dormitory with a torchlight and returned bearing midnight snacks! Rapunzel watched quietly. All was going well except two days after we started our raids, the captain-in-charge called me and three others out at the morning roll call and made us front roll on the grounds. For twenty whole minutes. It was puzzling to say the least. And it started happening every morning after our raids. How did he know?

Thanks to Rapunzel, I started many days with front rolls on the camp grounds. All for a few midnight snacks! We wondered who had been ratting us out and after five punishment-laden mornings, the snitch was finally discovered. Mona caught Rapunzel slipping a piece of paper under the door of the Captain's office, just before roll call.

But why would anyone do this? Perhaps she had a misplaced notion that by currying favour with the officer-in-charge, she would have a shot at getting the trophy at the end or she simply despised rule-breakers or perhaps she just didn't like our faces. But as the saying goes, snitches land in ditches, so we had our moment on the last night of the camp.

Rapunzel had painstakingly washed and blow-dried her hair that night as she had to take the the Army bus that left at the break of dawn. There was some dormitory gossip about a dishy boyfriend waiting for her at Rupa, a military base a few thousand feet short of Tawang. So as Rapunzel slept peacefully, dreaming about her upcoming romantic rendezvous, I squeezed an entire tube of toothpaste across the length of her hair. Now you can only imagine what transpired the next morning when she discovered her cascading tresses clumped together in a hot white mess. Rapunzel boarded the bus with her mucky hair hidden inside her hoodie and her face tear-streaked.

In the forces, you stood by your comrades through hell and back, so I didn't quite understand why anyone would betray their dorm-mates, which to me was a huge lapse of integrity and a sign of weak character, so I am not sure if I felt sorry for my actions at the time. But here I was, leech-ridden, badly bruised, hungry and lost, leading five others, wondering if the chickens had finally come home to roost and if all my pranking had brought me here, struggling to find a way home and hoping we did not get killed whilst doing so.

'There is nothing like that; it is all in your head,' Mike dismissed my speculations, but I wasn't too sure. I had, after all, incurred Charlie and Rapunzel's combined wrath just a few weeks ago.

P.S. Paraphrased from the words of the Greek philosopher Sextus Empiricus, 'The mills of the gods grind slowly, but they grind small.'

As I have gotten older, I also know that it is almost never an apples-to-apples comparison. A devious person might cheat another of his life savings, but divine justice does not mean he will lose the ill-begotten money, it means that he might suffer from chronic haemorrhoids or bad breath for the rest of his life, which is decidedly worse.

41

'WHAT DO WE DO NOW?' ROHIT ASKED, STARING AT THE mountains ahead. We had been ascending and descending for hours and getting nowhere. One mountain led to another and to another. There was no road or river in sight. It was an endless expanse of green all the way to the horizon. We could very well be on the other side of the long border that our country shared with China.

The uncertainty was dragging me down too and, for the first time that day, I felt pensive. I didn't know where we were going but I also knew we could not stop. The sun would set soon and we would be stranded in a jungle we knew little about – without food, gear, any form of protection or real survival skills. We simply wouldn't make it out alive, of that I was absolutely sure. Our options were limited and turning back wasn't one of them.

'We keep moving,' I said quietly, knowing well we were caught between a rock and a hard place. As before, we would go wherever the mountains took us and as fast as our legs could carry us.

Looking back, that day felt like a freefall from the top of a coniferous tree. We kept hitting pine needle after pine needle on our way down but never hit the ground. Caught in an endless loop of bristly branches, condemned to have our hopes dashed again and again and never getting anywhere near the Red Bridge. Being the oldest, I took the brunt of this excruciating endlessness.

Was the Jungle preparing me for life or just trying to break me?

42

'WHAT TIME WOULD IT BE?' ASKED MIKE, LOOKING UP AT THE sun. None of us knew. I felt like we had been walking for hours on end but without a working watch, it was hard to tell. It was, however, clear that we were way past the 1200 noon mark but the shifting cloud cover made it impossible to estimate accurately. What if we were still in the Jungle after last light?

Brushing the chilling thought aside, I turned to the five, 'The faster we move, the faster we reach home.'

The sun was known to set around 1815 hours and nothing but mountains lay ahead of us. 'As long as the sun is up, we are safe. So don't worry. We just have to walk faster,' I projected buoyantly.

The reticent Rohit added softly, 'I can try to guess the numbers of hours of daylight left.' Mike turned to him quizzically, 'How?'

'They taught us at an event but I don't know if it works,' Rohit replied with some hesitation.

I looked at Rohit, aghast, 'And you're telling us now? 'Why didn't you say so earlier??'

Rohit smiled sheepishly, 'I am not sure if it works,' to which I snapped impatiently, 'Doesn't mean we don't try it,' I growled with growing exasperation.

Mike's eyes darted at me as I read his expression. Sighing, I turned to Rohit, 'I am sorry, I ... er –' Rohit waved his hand; he understood my predicament, our collective predicament in fact.

'When we reach the top and I have a clear view of the sun, I'll try,' he added. I looked at the group and hollered, 'Let's go, let's go.' I had found a seemingly inconsequential purpose but it was not an entirely wasteful exercise so I doubled my pace. Knowledge of how much day light was left could help us plan and potentially save our lives. It was amazing how a sliver of hope could recharge your dying batteries.

'How do you check for daylight?' Neha asked quizzically.

'It's some old technique,' he replied. 'You place your four fingers against the sun and measure.' We looked on blankly as he continued, 'I'll show you when we have a clear view of the sun.'

Gigi, who was on Mona's back, stuck her hand out towards the sky and chirped, 'Like this, bhaiya?' Before Rohit could react, Gigi slipped off Mona's back and fell to the ground with a plop. As Neha reached out to pick her up, little Gigi got up, rubbing her behind and muttered, 'My tushie hurt.' The five of us burst into peels of laughter. It was the happy highlight of an otherwise inexplicably dark day. Her puppy-dog expression etched in my memory. *If I meet you again Gigi, I'll remind you of 'tushie' and 'mayomase'!*

Our banter made the ascent bearable.

'Tushie? Who taught you that word, Gigi?' I teased, to which Gigi replied matter-of-factly, 'Papa says it to mommy … put your tushie here, Mama, and she ...' 'Shut up, Gigi,' Mona cringed and shut her little sibling down while pulling her up a sharp incline. Not the response we had expected but children were known to innocently spill the beans. God knows we had all done it and heard hilarious stories from our parents when we were old enough to be shamed! *I, at the tender age of five, had once sung a bald man's song at a dinner party. And at the special request of my father's superior, who was bald as a coot. Apparently I was inspired by his bald pate and could think of no better song that evening. As you can imagine, that went well for my red-faced mother and silently chuckling father!*

Gigi's story made me chuckle and cringe, too. No one wanted to hear of their parents' shenanigans and, God forbid, if you had seen them more than canoodling. It was impossible to unsee that sort of stuff. You would need Dr Howard Mierzwiak from the movie *Eternal Sunshine of the Spotless Mind* to swipe our minds clean. After all, parents are just that … parents! The all-supreme Mother and Father meant to love us, nothing more, nothing less. And we'd been miraculously born out of thin air or the stork had dropped us into their nests. That is all we wanted to believe.

As we tittered over Gigi's revelations, Mike pointed towards the sun. We had been climbing for a while and were near the top, as the sun emerged from behind the clouds. It was time to test Rohit's technique.

We looked on in anticipation as Rohit stuck his hand towards the sun, as far as it would go. 'My top finger is right under the sun,' he said, moving his palm down, until his hand was straight in line with the horizon, counting as he went down. '1300 … 1400 ... 1500 … 1600 ... 1700 … Rohit tried it again, this time a bit more meticulously. Exactly the same result.

'It's roughly 1700 hours,' he said, trying hard to conceal the panic in his voice.

'Are you sure?' Mike asked sharply.

'The height of the four fingers is roughly one hour and I've measured five lengths of it from the bottom of the sun,' Rohit said.

We looked on, not quite understanding, when he added, 'You can tell the numbers of hours of light left by seeing how many four-finger sections you can get between the bottom of the sun and the horizon.' We let out a collective 'Ahh' and then there was silence.

This was anything but good news.

I quickly stuck my palm right under the sun and measured down to the perceived horizon. 1300 ... 1400 ... 1500 … 1600 … 1700 ... 1745? I turned to Rohit in panic. 'That's nearly 1800 hours! Sun sets around 1815.'

'Your hand is smaller, and the time could be off by half an hour but –' his voice trailed off. There was hushed silence again.

Best case scenario, we had ninety minutes of light left. Worst case, about an hour … and then who knows what was waiting for us … aka *The Blair Witch Project*! And we didn't even have a camcorder to document our story for posterity.

And if this was not enough, we were yet to meet *the secret enemy in the hills.* A pesky little creature known to take the best of soldiers down.

P.S. Tik-tok, tik-tok, tik-tok! Time was ticking like a bomb. The Jungle was watching all our moves and planning its next. The near-drowning, leeches, the bruises, lightning strike, the hunger, the chopper that did not spot us, the villagers who did not help; every single setback was throbbing like an open wound. And underneath all this din, I could hear the voice inside my head: we must save the little ones.

43

HUMAN WILL FAR OUTWEIGHS HUMAN SKILLS. IF YOU HAVE got the will, the skill will follow. It is a no-brainer. And, perhaps, this is why so much has been said and written about the power of indomitable will and spirit.

In the world of sports, this perhaps rings the truest for boxing. Boxers who have achieved greatness in the ring often talk about how their unalloyed willpower emboldens them to take on and trump a technically superior fighter. The classic David versus Goliath metaphor. If you can visualize defeating your opponent before you enter the ring, you will defeat him in the ring. That is the power of the mind and its ensuing will, as captured in the inspirational poem by William Ernest Henley. Henley wrote it during his darkest hour, when physical and mental agony were threatening to destroy his will.

INVICTUS

Out of the night that covers me,
Black as the pit from pole to pole,
I thank whatever gods may be
For my unconquerable soul.

In the fell clutch of circumstance
I have not winced nor cried aloud.
Under the bludgeonings of chance
My head is bloody, but unbowed.

Beyond this place of wrath and tears
Looms but the Horror of the shade,
And yet the menace of the years
Finds and shall find me unafraid.

It matters not how strait the gate,
How charged with punishments the scroll,
I am the master of my fate,
I am the captain of my soul.

We were living through exactly that kind of day: the unforeseeable circumstances, the bludgeonings, the wrath of nature and the relentless punishments. The Jungle was an all-powerful being in front of us and the end to our ordeal was nowhere in sight.

As the six of us stared at the mountain ahead of us and the hours of daylight remaining, I knew there was no option but to push harder, climb faster, keep my eyes open and throw out any anxiety I was feeling in the moment. It was a race to the finish now. We had to make it out alive. And it was not something I was saying to myself consciously. My head was bloody, proverbially, but I would not let the Jungle douse my soul.

It was all lofty and good until we entered a denser part of the Jungle during the ascent and heard the unmistakable gushing sound of water.

The home to what we know now as the mighty little *Dim-Dims* ...

P.S. Expecting the Jungle to not have a trick or two up its sleeve was like expecting a scorpion not to sting. No creature could go against its own nature. The Jungle was no exception.

44

WITHOUT DISCUSSING THE 'WHYS' AND 'WHAT-IFS', WE started to descend towards the sound of water. Coming from somewhere not too far off, and unlike the soothing babbling brooks we had encountered during our endless ascents and descents, the water was crashing hard against the ground.

Like moths to a fly, we moved in its direction. It did not even cross our minds that we had escaped the treacherous rivulet at the start of the day and decided to seek refuge in the mountains instead. Instinctively, we moved towards the sound of the waterfall.

'I am tired,' Gigi whined, her big eyes droopy with hunger and fatigue.

'You're a strong girl, Gigi, and strong girls do not get tired,' I said firmly as we moved in a row. The descent was steep and the path was strewn with rocks and shrubs. Knowing how long we had until sundown was helping me stay focused and, given the terrain, we had to tread carefully, lest we landed spreadeagled in some ravine. So we lumbered on silently, thinking of nothing other than our escape from this mess.

'I am hungry,' Gigi whined as she walked slowly. Sensing an incoming tantrum, Mona looked at Gigi and shot a terse, 'Do you want to see Mommy and Daddy tonight or should I leave you in the jungle?' Gigi shrivelled her face, ready to cry.

'Stop it, Gigi,' Mona snapped and hoisted Gigi onto her back. 'We'll eat when we get home,' she added softly. I sighed and kept walking. There was no time for introspection or procrastination anymore. Time, much like the Jungle, was not on our side.

The descent was faster and we had hit the bottom of the valley only to realize that the sound was still some distance away. I looked at the five and motioned that we keep moving.

'Oh!' Neha suddenly pointed to my left arm with horror. My arms were still bleeding. 'Don't!' I warned her to look away. The last thing we needed was my younger sibling passing out on us, again. When I looked down at both my arms, I was a surprised at the lack of pain. For the number of bloody gashes and leech lesions across my arms, I should have been bawling. Instead I felt nothing, not even the throb of a fresh wound.

The adrenaline rush explained it. They say if you take your mind away from the site of pain, it stops you from thinking about it. What else can explain how battle-hardened soldiers handle pain? And how they are prepared for torture if they are ever caught behind enemy lines. This was no comparison whatsoever, though.

'The sound is coming from up there,' Mike said pointing to our left, at the mountain. 'Let's go,' I said and started to climb diagonally towards it, holding Neha's hand tightly. The sunlight had greatly diminished. So Rohit's daylight hours technique seemed alarmingly accurate.

As we commenced our ascent with vigour, Rohit overtook me as the leader of the group and Mike fell to the back. I am not sure if we knew what we were hoping to find but it seemed like our only option.

The creatures of the Jungle were starting to come alive. Crickets, for one, were chirping like their life depended on it. Oddly, it did. Ensnaring the missus to procreate, they were having a field day. If someone were to get the decibel meter to the Jungle right now, these noisy creatures would have been fined for noise pollution. Something howled and made our hair stand on end but we kept moving ahead. We had seen enough today and put a lot of things behind us too. Fear included. 'That's some monkey,' I added cheekily while stretching my hand out to pull Neha up. 'Do not look,' I warned again as she looked at my battered arm.

The banter, the inner monologue, every conversation we could have, even the ones within were put on hold. We were focused on the ascent and climbing fast. The sound of the water grew louder every few hundred metres, giving us hope and purpose.

Another screech and howl reverberated in the Jungle. Had a monkey escaped from the clutches of a hungry carnivore? Perhaps. Other than Gigi's periodic gasps, we did not pause. We could ill-afford anything that slowed us down. Maybe the waterbody we were inching towards was a watering hole for the feral beasts of the jungle. I did not give much thought to it as the gushing sound got louder.

'We're close,' I said softly and kept moving. Rohit was clearing the way for us with my stick as we pushed through the shrubs and foliage. Neha was right behind me, sticking to me like a shadow, wanting to protect me from whatever lay ahead. Younger, but always wiser. With the approaching dusk, the Jungle felt more alive, its nocturnal creatures coming out of slumber and making their presence felt. The screeches, howls, barking, chirping and the occasional hiss performed in chorus like an eerie concerto. The Jungle was preparing to unleash its next round of salvos at us.

And just like that, we arrived there. Gushing and falling with a lot of force was a small waterfall, and we did not know at the time that it was the breeding ground for a certain kind of fly which was known to cause havoc in the region. As we stopped to evaluate our options, the deadly little flies, breeding in its running waters, started to bite us. Within minutes, the site of the bites on our bodies, started throbbing with pain and swelled up. They were biting through thick fabric too and spared no one.

We could not stop here, even if we had wanted to. Any hope that the sound of the water would show us a way home were unfounded and misplaced. There was no miracle waiting for us. With the sun less than an hour from setting, and plunging the Jungle and us into absolute darkness, we had no option but to keep moving up.

This was our darkest hour.

A shrill screech echoed, sending shivers down our spines. It was the Jungle speaking to us in code.

'Looking busy, getting nowhere, eh?' the Jungle mocked.

It was right …

45

DRAWING IN A DEEP BREATH, I CONTINUED. A PALL OF GLOOM was hanging around us as we followed the water upstream. At our wit's end and for dearth of a better idea, we had started to follow it.

The ascent was the steepest we had encountered thus far, and our reserves of energy were at their lowest but every time I felt close to giving up, my subconscience played my resolve on loop: *Whatever happens, we must save the little ones.*

It was a strange mix of despondency and steely resolve. Every cell in my body was fighting to survive the day. It was probably the same for the rest, except they were not carrying the Coleridgian albatross around their necks of leading the six of us to a sure-shot tragedy and four families into an emotional abyss forever. Deep guilt and a deeper burden still. There was an acute self-awareness and desperation driving me, but nothing had worked so far. The Jungle and its inexorable pull were greater than anything I had imagined. The only saving grace was that no one had accused me yet. For that, I am grateful to this day.

'A few more metres, Gigi,' Neha said softly as the youngest among us was ready to break. She was not the only one. I was feeling it in my bones: the enormous weight of the day.

'We get to the top and then we rest, Gigi, okay?' I said, forcing myself to smile for her sake. Mike was leading us now and every now and then, pulling me up some sharp incline. There were plenty on this leg of our misadventure. The Jungle might have ripped my shirt in many places but it had spared my boots. So pushing my foot firmly into the ground, I kept climbing.

'Are you okay?' I asked Neha softly, who nodded and asked me the same. I smiled weakly but said nothing more. I couldn't see my own, but her face bore signs of exhaustion. To see her lose hope was crushing but I had to brush it aside and focus ahead. I pulled her up and she pulled up Gigi. Together, we continued to climb, hoping to put the nightmare to an end.

'I want to go home,' Gigi suddenly burst into violent tears and started to shake convulsively. Her cries brought a lump in my throat and we stopped. Mona hugged her tightly, 'We are going home, Gigi,' her own voice trembling with pain.

'My mother read a story by Rudyard Kipling to me once,' Rohit said suddenly. 'It was about this brave little child who lived in the Jungle.' To which Mona quickly added, 'Are you talking about Mowgli?'

Rohit smiled and nodded, 'Yes, Mowgli. Have you heard of Mowgli, Gigi?' Gigi looked up and shook her tear-stained face from side to side.

'Come, let me tell you,' Rohit said, as he put Gigi on his back. 'Hold on tightly, it is a thrilling adventure.'

I sighed as Gigi clung to Rohit tightly and we started to climb again. Managing a six-year-old needed constant innovativeness. God knows we had tried it all day. Also, none of Gigi's 'tantrums', if we could even call them that, were of her own doing.

'So little Mowgli was lost by his parents as a baby in a jungle and he was then adopted by a mother-wolf called Raksha and a father-wolf called Rama …'

Gigi listened in rapt attention, 'Then?'

'There was a jungle tiger called Sher Khan who demanded that Raksha and Rama give him the little baby but the wolves refused,' Rohit continued.

Gigi's curiosity was piqued. She asked, 'Did Sher Khan eat Mowgli?'

Rohit negotiated a steep incline carefully and replied, 'No, Gigi. Sher Khan could not, and so little Mowgli grew up with the pack, hunting with his brother wolves.'

'Woooow!' Gigi said with childlike wonder, having completely forgotten her emotional breakdown a few minutes ago. And what a relief that was, even momentarily.

As Rohit continued to regale little Gigi, we kept ascending steadily along the thin stream. Thinking of nothing but what lay a few feet ahead, and with my hunter knife in one hand, I pulled Neha up with the other. My arms were starting to itch really bad. It was probably from the insect bites near the waterfall below. Mona and Neha were scratching themselves on their legs. The sneaky vermin had gotten in through their pants and stung them too.

Sometimes ignorance is bliss! None of us knew at the time that these bites could cause serious inflammations. 'Tuck your socks over your pants,' I said, and they did. Gigi's hoodie was pulled on. Mike and Rohit were scratching themselves too.

'This is just unbelievable,' I muttered angrily. I was ranting away at the Jungle, *When nothing else works, you send these little bugs to kill us? Really? Shame on you!*

I let off steam, internally, of course, and continued the ascent. We could not see the sun but judging by the light, it was moments away from setting. I was trying hard not to think about it and focus on the steep climb ahead.

'Look,' Neha said with gusto. All of us craned our necks to look in the general direction and realized we were a few metres from the top. I let out a cry of relief and a prayer and ran up on the double, panting.

The sun was very close to the horizon when I reached the top. The skies had taken on a brilliant molten hue, the diaphanous clouds refracting a blazing orange everywhere. As I scanned the vistas slowly, an overwhelming feeling rose in the pit of my stomach.

I wanted to scream but my voice was stuck inside, overwhelmed. My pupils dilated as I turned to look at the others, wildly gesticulating. My lips were moving but words remained trapped inside. I squinted my eyes hard and looked again, to ensure I was not hallucinating. But it was unmistakable.

Through the trees and the foliage, I saw the metal structure. It was right there, at the bottom of the mountain, glistening in the light of the dying sun. Our Red Bridge!

P.S. It is always the darkest just before the day dawneth. *It may sound silly but write this down somewhere. I will vouch for it.*

46

THE SIX OF US STOOD IN STUPEFIED SILENCE LOOKING AT the Red Bridge below. While we were expecting another curveball, the misadventure had unexpectedly ended.

It was over! The end had arrived as suddenly as its beginning earlier that morning.

After momentary disbelief, the impact of our discovery sank in. Little Gigi started jumping up and down singing, 'Red Bridge, Red Bridge' while Mona and Rohit hugged each other spontaneously. It was an ecstatic moment for all of us. Neha squeezed my hand comfortingly, just as Mike put his arm around my neck.

In that moment, I felt everything and nothing, all at once. The Albatross around my neck seemed to have disappeared, leaving an aching numbness in its place. I should have thrust my hands in the air and screamed triumphantly, at the top of my lungs.

I am the master of my fate
I am captain of my soul

I could not, I did not.

Without a compass, a watch or a chaperone, without food, any means of protecting ourselves or any meaningful understanding of survival in one of the harshest terrains, we had made it out alive. And relatively unscathed.

'*Whatever happens …*' rang in my ears. But with a quieter, less urgent feeling. The storm had passed and every single one of us had survived it and possibly changed by it.

'Don't sit,' I said sharply as Mona and Gigi sat down on other haunches, wanting to take a break. 'If the sun sets before we reach the bridge, we'll lose our bearing,' I added cautiously.

As the sky was still ablaze with the colours of the setting sun, the six of us started our final descent towards the Red Bridge.

Had the Jungle shown mercy and released us or had we persisted with such fierce doggedness that we had defeated it? Had the very waters that nearly drowned Gigi and me finally come to our rescue?

Truthfully, if we hadn't climbed towards the waterfall and followed the water all the way to its source near the top, we might never have reached this vantage point; the Red Bridge would have been lost to us forever and we, to the Jungle.

Purely on instinct and with a whole lot of good luck, we'd found our way out. We were going home.

The final descent was made in low light conditions and hence we moved with abundant caution. We'd roughly chalked out a more or less linear path to the Red Bridge below, unless the Jungle had something up its sleeve again. I was not willing to entrust it with our lives yet.

I'd believe we had won only when we reached the bridge alive and in one piece. I was also hoping to have a vehicle from the base waiting for us but given the kind of day we had had, my expectations were low. Hope for the best, plan for the worst. And the worst-case scenario was to camp on the side of the bridge and flag down the first vehicle coming our way.

'I am going to eat chicken momos when I get home tonight,' Mona said with salivating surety. There was a little local eatery just off the base that prepared the most delectable dumplings so it was within the realm of possibility to imagine the foods we would be consuming tonight. But I just wasn't counting my chickens before they were hatched. The Jungle could upstage us at any time so I kept my guards up, focussing on the five feet ahead of us.

In silence and with absolute purpose, we started our final descent. The backs of my hands were itching like they were on fire. Mona and Neha too were scratching their shins vigorously. But we trudged on. Rohit and me leading, followed by Gigi and Neha and tail-ended by Mona and Mike.

The crickets were creating a cacophonous shindy loud enough to drown all thoughts. Screeches, howls, barks, hissing. The Jungle was alive and awake, and you could put nothing past it. I was sorely aware of this and was silently saying whatever prayers came to my mind.

The last leg of any unintended adventure was the trickiest. Emotionally, everyone's guards were down and there was a natural tendency to be lax. It was most crucial to keep it together at this point but sometimes there is only that much you can do.

As we neared the base of the mountain, the sound of the river below become audible and overshadowed the jungle-din around us. A pleasant sound by all means. The day was coming to an end finally, but we still had a few more metres to descend. Owing to its proximity to the river or perhaps it has rained, the bed of the Jungle was moist. 'Walk slowly, watch every step, the ground is really wet,' I warned the group.

And then, I slipped.

Rolling down a few metres, I fell on my knees. A sharp twinge emanated from my left knee. My pant was torn, and the skin under it had a gash, blood gushing from it.

Damn you! Damn you! Damn you!

As I slowly sat up, I was raging like a mad bull inside, hurling the choicest profanities at the Jungle. What deviousness!

Even in its final moments with us, whilst releasing us from its vice-like grip, it had extracted a pound of flesh and dropkicked me! Imagine the guile! The Jungle had insidiously waited till the very last minute to deliver a final uppercut, gorilla-style.

Something to remember me by, darling!

Mike pulled me up and holding onto him and Neha, I limped down towards the bridge. I believe I let out a cryptic little laugh at my particular situation, my knee bleeding and throbbing with pain.

As we arrived at the base of the mountain, I stared at the Red Bridge, its large structure looming over the six small humans. The sun had dipped right behind it, leaving a purple hue in the sky. Purple like the bruises the Jungle had given us.

It was finally over but not quite …

47

I STARED IMPASSIVELY AT THE ONE-TONNE TRUCK PARKED NEAR the bridge, its yellow indicator lights furtively blinking.

We had faced so many hurdles on our way that when the end came, it crept in quietly. Despite the physical injuries and fatigue, I felt neither joy nor sorrow. Not even relief. My mind swirled in an idiosyncratic mix of emotions and numbness at the same time. A deluge of tears threatened to breach the dam, but they did not.

The Red Bridge, the centre of my last picnic and summer in Tawang, was in front of us but I felt nothing for it, except a little misplaced contempt. In hindsight, I also understood what it meant to be emotionally detached, from victory and failure too. The Jungle had made us go through hell, but it had taught us lessons for the rest of our lives.

The large Red Bridge looked dark and ominous and nothing like what I had imagined at the start of the day. The journey to get to it had been so surreal and momentous that the bridge now appeared insignificant in comparison. Perhaps, something inside me had permanently shifted or I was beyond caring. The river gushed beneath the bridge, its rumble reverberating in the valley. For a split second, the memory of my near-drowning rushed back and sent a shiver down my spine. I had had enough of the water for one day.

But the day was over. It was finally over.

The mission to survive had been accomplished. I had kept the promise I made to myself or maybe the Jungle had had its share of fun and released us when it got weary of us. Not without giving me a final kick though on my way out! A grand reminder of who the boss was!

I looked at the rescue party of four who were waiting for us near the truck. Apparently, they had been waiting there for many hours. I noticed a little campfire on the side with the sturdy matte silver Army kettle brewing tea over it. Smoke rose from the little pit they had dug up to brew fresh tea.

One of them examined my arms and deftly removed the leeches off them. He rolled up my torn sleeves, dabbing both my arms with betadine and covered the cuts and bruises with antiseptic cream and cotton gauze. I drew his attention to my messed up left knee and he cringed at the mass of flesh hanging from it. '*Aap toh jung ladd ke aye ho, didi,*' he said lightly while sitting down to examine the mangled knee. (A battlefield, eh?) He was right. Today had, as a matter of fact, felt nothing less than a battle for the six of us. A battle to make it out alive. Warning me of the impending pain that awaited me and before I could react, he overturned the bottle of betadine antiseptic on my knee. It stung badly as the thick brown antiseptic solution ran over my wound and down my pant and boots, staining both. Then he squeezed the antiseptic cream on it and waited to see if the bleeding had stopped. My hands were itching but there was nothing they could do. '*Doctor sahib ko dikhana*,' he added with concern, exchanging a glance with the man brewing tea, who muttered under his breath, 'Dim-dim.' They probably wanted the doctor at the base to check if there were indeed the bitemarks of the dim-dim. And hoping they weren't.

Mike and Rohit were tended to next for bruises and leeches. Somehow, the physical toll was lower on both. Neha and Mona had no bruises except the bitemarks on their legs and a few leeches. And except the initial debacle in the rivulet, the horrors of the Jungle had mostly spared little Gigi. No surprises there. Everyone loved Gigi!

As we were accounted for and tended to, the co-driver pulled the kettle off the fire and poured freshly brewed tea into white metal mugs and handed one to each of us. A couple of Parle-G packets were ripped open and we were goaded to drink tea to boost our energy.

I watched Neha slowly slurp the hot tea and wolf down biscuits. Tears welled up in my eyes. Her resilience and grit baffled me. Not once during the entire day had my sibling complained or whined except when she saw me in peril. What had I put them all through!

'Thank you, bhaiya,' Neha said gratefully as she gorged on the biscuits like I had never seen before.

The driver looked on empathetically and almost apologetically. If they had known we were this hungry, they would have brought a proper meal along, he rued, seeing how everyone had attacked the biscuits.

Guilt-ridden and overwhelmed, I refused the refreshments. I had no appetite and felt a peculiar emptiness inside. All I wanted was to curl up inside my bed and sleep, treating the day like the nightmare it had been.

As the five indulged in the joys of Parle-G biscuits and freshly made campfire chai, the driver radioed back to base, '*Jai Hind sir, bachhe mil gaye hain.*' That the kids had been found was announced and the radio set in the vehicle crackled. An indecipherable voice at the other end acknowledged the message.

He signed off saying they were heading back to the base before setting the radio down. The sun had set right behind the mountain as we climbed the back of the truck. Gigi hauled in first, followed by Neha, Mona, Rohit and Mike.

Mike and the danda-man hauled me up into the vehicle last and I still recall feeling my knees buckling under me. I was the last one to get in and settle down near the door; my left leg stretched out, staring out into the twilight sky. There was pindrop silence as the truck took off towards the base.

To this day, I don't know fully well what had transpired back at the base when the news of us gone missing came to light. I was told later that the replacement truck dropped men at the spot of the breakdown, (from where we had descended) in search of us. Of course, they didn't find us, we had been long gone but they continued their search and instead found two metal tiffin boxes entangled in the waterside foliage downstream. They were Mona's. I suspect they must have been relieved to not have found any bodies, which, incidentally, was not unheard of in the region.

At the same time, another truck was dispatched straight to the Red Bridge where it waited for us in the fervent hope that we would find our way to our picnic spot. Thankfully, the best men had been sent to bring us back home safely.

Given the poor visibility, the vehicle literally crawled back to base, negotiating the mountain roads as deftly as possible. We could ill-afford any more mishaps!

My mind drifted aimlessly as I looked out into the valley. There were no thoughts of any consequence, just a numbness or a jamboree of what-ifs. I guess the magnitude of what we had endured simply had not sunk in yet. I had handled more than I could fathom, more than I was ready to confront.

The others were silent too. We were all suffering from post-traumatic stress or maybe that would hit us later. This was just a shock-induced silence.

Mike and I held hands momentarily. I did not care if anyone was looking. We had survived a monster of a day and I would have bitten anyone's head off for objecting!

I fixed my eyes on Neha, who was seated on the opposite side with Gigi. She looked back at me and smiled reassuringly. *We've made it*, I read it in her eyes and looked away post-haste. My younger sister, who looked up to me, did not need to see that I was on the brink of crumbling.

It was a long drive back, the air reeking of uncomfortable silence and the occasional sound of water gushing below. The aches and pains were coming back with feral ferocity. Now that the adrenaline rush had been replaced by silence and inactivity, the bites and gashes and wounds were collectively attacking my body, every pain receptor in hyperdrive.

As far as I was concerned, it had been an apocalyptic day, but it was over. Tragedy had been averted not once, but twice.

We had all survived and that surely meant something …

What happened next did too!

48

AS THE RATTLING ONE-TONNE ENTERED THE BASE, GIGI, WHO had fallen asleep, got up and started to clap, pulling me out of my numb stupor instantly. Neha quietly got up from the other side and sat next to me silently. We were home and all was well.

It was dark already, the lights lining the roads were switched on. Our ride climbed the hill, crossed the well-lit officers' mess, which was expertly constructed on a slope and descended to the barracks – a row of rooms for all the officers living on the base.

We had left around 0500 hours in the morning but it felt like an eternity. Perhaps, a small part inside me had felt we were never going to make it back. A lot of emotions were churning within me, working at cross purposes. But numbness was no longer one of them. We had made it back. That was cause enough to celebrate.

As the truck pulled into the barracks area and ground to a halt, I saw the mothers standing in line. All four of them. The overhead lights lit the area well but the expression on their faces was inscrutable.

On seeing my mother, I felt a surge of emotion. I wanted to hug her tight and tell her all that had happened to us. I wanted to maybe sob a little. There were so many things I wanted to say and apologize for. I was still gathering my thoughts when the danda-man pulled out the hooks of the door and threw it open. Sitting closest to the gate, I got up first but with my left leg awfully stiff, I had to be helped down. Mike and Rohit got off next, followed by Neha, Gigi and Mona.

Taking a deep breath, I looked at the others. There was relief and excitement in everyone's eyes. We were safe, we were home. The ordeal was over.

The six of us walked towards our waiting mothers with great anticipation. I, with my predilection to underplay injuries, did not let on the knee injury. There was no point adding further to their misery but the condition of my knee did not go unnoticed. My mother caught it instantly, like she always did.

As we got closer, I saw my mother's face. Her expression was a little disconcerting. The ladies should have been over the moon but they looked on impassively! I shot a quick glance at Mike and Rohit who were walking alongside, while the other three were behind us. Something was not right.

As we reached them, Gigi, Mona and Neha overtook us and slunk past our mothers without uttering a word. *Rather odd.* I looked at my mother and could clearly see anguish in her eyes. So without uttering a word, I threw my arms around her and hugged her tight.

Almost simultaneously, Mike and Rohit were smacked across their faces in full public view.

Wait, what? No, no, no! Not them!

P.S. Two days after the adventure, when we were all allowed to meet, I apologized to Mike and Rohit for the grand homecoming bestowed upon them by their mothers. The violent slap across Mike and Rohit's faces stung me more than the wounds inflicted by the Jungle. There was a moment of silence before our eyes met. Then we burst out cackling. We laughed so hard that we cried!

49

Flashback
Officers' Mess, few hours ago

WHILE WE WERE FIGHTING THE JUNGLE OFF, THE MOTHERS had learnt of the adventure and converged in panic. All four of them.

Word had gone around and Pinkie auntie was duly questioned. The distraught ladies demanded to know why she hadn't chaperoned us and her (inexplicable) reason for choosing to inform the children about her last-minute change of plans instead of the mothers.

'The baked beans from the night before had done me in but I sent them a note. How would I know they would push off without a chaperone?' she argued. 'Baked beans? Were they on the menu last night?' Mona's mother enquired. In the ensuing commotion, the menu card from the previous night's dinner was procured. Baked beans were not on the menu!

Now, even if our appointed chaperone had indeed helped herself to a bucket full of those succulent tomato sauce-flavoured beans, she could not explain away her reasons for informing the children instead of their mothers. Pinkie auntie was duly pulled up for being irresponsible, but the damage was done.

We were untraceable and our mothers had spent the better part of the day in nerve-wracking anxiety. Imagining the worst-case scenario while the search parties were dispatched to look for us.

I reckon my mother was the worst-affected. News had arrived via Ram Niwas, the driver, and Barua – our danda-man – that her elder daughter had dismissed their advice and led the group down to the stream. For my mother, it would have been hard to understand, leave alone explain away that sort of recklessness, especially with five other lives at stake. And more so, without having me around to defend myself.

I could not have defended myself. Deep down, I knew that if anyone deserved that grand reception of a slap, it was me!

While we were struggling to find our way back, the mothers had huddled together, waiting for news about us, praying we'd get home safe. The harshness of the terrain wasn't lost on them, nor was the treacherous weather. When the rescue party team leader radioed back to base, 'Jai Hind sir, bachhe mil gaye hain,' they had sighed in relief. They had promptly decided to give us the grand homecoming reception! Except only two of them went ahead with it!

My mangled knee had saved my face, literally.

EPILOGUE

AN HOUR AFTER RETURNING TO BASE, THE MEDICAL OFFICER bandaged my left knee, dressed the wounds on my arms and administered an anti-allergy shot. My hands still itched all over and the bite marks had turned a deeper red. Mike and Rohit's bruises were tended too, and Neha and Mona got a shot each for the same itch. 'You kids had some day!' the officer joked. It wasn't funny but I kept silent!

Thankfully, the Jungle did not leave us thirsty, so no one was dehydrated. Minor mercies!

Later that night, my father listened with rapt attention as I narrated our ordeal, blow by blow. Neha nodded alongside to corroborate it. 'You've been brave but always remember, discretion is the better part of valour. We will always have your back but you had your mother really worried,' he said and went back to his late night calls and files without letting us in on the serious repercussions had the day ended in tragedy.

A year later, as we were reminiscing about Tawang, my father had remarked matter-of-factly, 'You took full responsibility and didn't give up. It takes a lot of courage to do that. I am proud of you.' His words ring in my ears to this day ...

But that night, I could not sleep. The events of the day had just started to sink in and I was still reeling in shock and disbelief. Had all of this craziness happened to me? Had I just made my greatest memory? Had the Jungle imparted what no classroom ever could? Yes, yes and yes! Even that night, I knew I would treasure this day forever.

A few days later, during the last get-together of the officers' wives at the base, my mother was duly advised, 'Girls should behave like girls. Rein her in.' My mother was silent.

Might I gleefully and gratefully report that she took the 'advice' and tossed it out.

P.S. My left knee was scarred that day, a little cross etched into it. And as I pen the last chapter of my glorious adventure, I look down at it and smile.

Me: Ha!

Jungle: Ha ha!

LESSONS FROM THE JUNGLE … (OF LIFE, FOR LIFE) …

SOME OF THESE LESSONS MIGHT SEEM CONTRADICTORY, offensive or downright inane, but semantics be damned, if you've gotten this far in the book, I am hoping you'll understand the spirit behind them.

- Go on adventures while you are still in your teens. They will reveal to you who you really are, and on the off-chance that you don't like what it uncovers, there will be enough time for you to course-correct.
- Jungles are living entities, whimsical and eccentric. Don't mess with a jungle, I repeat! I'd go one melodramatic step further and implore you to pray to them like the Navi. If you don't know who Navis are, refer to the 2009 film, *Avatar*. Jungles can kill you; they can make you too.
- Take a leap of faith. If you survive, you'll have great stories to tell and if you don't, well too bad. You will, in the very least, become a headline on page 36. Who is getting out alive anyway?

- Hope for the best, plan for the worst. Don Quixote never won a war and if God forbid, he's your hero, you won't either.
- Be open to advice but take your own decisions! And if the decision is yours and you fall on your face, well you can't assign the blame on someone else. And if it's right ... hooray! Go ahead and gloat! Till you fall on your face, and you will. Life is a cycle.
- Be watchful of signs. They can be tricky. The universe doesn't always give you signs, but when it does, you should duly register. Sometimes, it gives you what you want. And then may the Lord save you! (Be careful what you wish for.)
- Don't believe everything you see. Mirages fool the best of us.
- Never underestimate the force of water, even when its still. Learn how to swim as early as possible in life but don't expect not to drown. The strongest swimmers often take on the most turbulent waters and drown! Basically, waters are not to be trifled with!
- Take a few knocks, let a few leeches suck your blood! Who needs dirty blood anyway? Let your opponent have a go at your solar plexus, it's a great workout for the core!
- Don't underestimate the power of failure. It keeps you humble and hungry; besides, even your enemies deserve happiness!

- To girls, learn martial arts! This life hack can save your life. Besides courage and confidence, it also gives you an illusion of invincibility. In a world that is all about posturing, this illusion or delusion will save you!
- Nothing risked, nothing gained. Push your boundaries and step outside comfort zones, but if you jump off a plane without a parachute, don't except miracles. Those stunts only work in the Stan Lee Universe. Take calculated risks.
- Carry some food and water every time you leave home. One meal in the tummy, one for the road. Amidst pandemics, earthquakes, floods and political mayhem, you never know when you'll get home and if that home will be standing exactly where you left it!
- It is not necessary to capture every memory through photographs, unless you want to delude the world about your perfect life! Some of the best memories you're ever going to make take place when the camera isn't pointing at you. Breathe and put that selfie stick away!
- Expect the unexpected. Once this expectation is set, there is nothing unexpected! Voila!
- Don't wear camouflage gear to a jungle unless you're playing *Terminator* or you're a soldier. Fluorescent pinks, yellows and oranges, please.

- Adventures will find you if you are truly lucky. They are great teachers and agents of revelations and transformations! Cherish them, even if they nearly killed you!
- Don't take yourself too seriously. Laugh a little when your luck is down. That is what you will remember the most when you're back on the saddle.
- Persist, persist, persist. It's not over until it's over!

TIPS FOR SURVIVAL IN THE MOUNTAINS AND JUNGLES

WHETHER IN JUNGLES, ON MOUNTAINS OR BOTH, IT IS entirely possible to lose one's way – always hope for the best but plan for the worst. This planning entails grit, ingenuity, calm and some basic survival knowledge and skills.

If you got the first three covered, the fourth and fifth are easy and while there are various tips, checklists and methods that are available across online channels, I am listing the simplest ones I found which have resonated with me, whilst you come up with yours in the due course of your own adventures.

- Never go into the mountains or wilderness alone.
- Make sure your backpack has all necessary supplies for travel and also things that could come in handy if you get lost or injured.
- Each member of the party should have a compact water filter system and/or water purification tablets.

- Bring an emergency blanket and a tarp to stay warm.
- The best plans are made well ahead of time and compared with detailed trail maps. Include information from professionals who have travelled in the area; including any landmarks in the area and what dangers you can expect.
- While hiking, every so often, look behind you. This will help you remember what the route looks like on the way back home.
- Take some photos of the route. Include pictures with your hand pointing in the direction to go when heading back home. Try to include landmarks located near the trail.
- If you become concerned with not being able to find your way home, make some arrows on the ground with loose rocks or branches.
- In the event you're lost, don't panic. The last thing you want to do is go thrashing around further away from a viable trail or deeper into the mountain wilderness. If it is getting late in the day and you are in a safe area, it may be best to make camp and get a good night's rest before starting again in the morning.
- If you feel you are lost, do not start running or walking faster than your normal pace. If you do, you risk the chance of falling in the mountainous terrain and injuring yourself.
- Never split from the group or split the group up. If you do so, the rescue party will be looking for two groups of people instead of one.

- Relax and think: How did you get here? What landmarks should you be able to see? What was the direction of travel? What was the last-known position where you were sure you were on the right trail?
- Observe: What does the terrain look like? Where on the map does it look like that? What is the sun's location in the sky? How much time is left before sunset? What is left in the supply inventory? How long will the supplies last?
- Plan: Never move from this area until you have a plan. Even though phones may not work deep in the mountains, you may be lucky enough to have coverage. If you can get a signal, call for help. Try to signal other hikers in the area by blowing a whistle three times (this is the international distress signal.) If you are trying to signal to aircraft, try using a mirror, put on bright-coloured clothing, or arrange objects to spell out HELP or SOS in an area where someone in a plane or helicopter can spot them.
- If you are carrying a flare gun, shoot a flare when an approaching aircraft is coming towards you. When the flare is seen, the aircraft will circle you to let you know that you have been spotted.
- In case someone is injured, look for a sheltered spot to keep you out of the rain and wind before it gets dark. Use the tarps and emergency blankets to make a tent to sleep in. Ideally, someone on the group should be trained in how to handle medical emergencies.

Don't sleep near large water bodies. The noise might make it hard to hear the rescuers. Carefully start a controlled fire for warmth and to help signal your location to rescuers. Hang colourful items from the backpacks on trees and bushes to help rescuers find you.

- If in the event your one-day hike turns into a long disaster, it will be advantageous to know how to start a fire, build a shelter, find or secure safe drinking water, determine what is safe to eat, signal for help, and hunt, trap, or fish for food.
- In the mountains, keep moving straight until you reach running water. This is simply because, in the mountains, communities are located around water supplies. Finding a river or creek and following it may lead you to a small town. Always follow the water downstream. At some point, you will cross a road or a road junction. Following the water downstream will also eventually take you back to more populated areas.

OTHER SURVIVAL HACKS

Telling directions without a compass

DURING THE DAY, TRY THE SHADOW-STICK METHOD TO track the sun's shadow. When the sun is approximately in the middle of the sky, push a one-metre-long stick into the ground and mark the tip of its shadow with a small rock or a small stick. Ensure the ground is absolutely flat and clear of vegetation. As the sun moves east to west in the sky, the shadow of the stick will move west to east. Wait for fifteen minutes and you'll see that the shadow has moved. Place another rock or small stick to mark the new shadow. Repeat again after fifteen minutes. Then place a long stick connecting the three rocks until that line becomes a clear west-to-east line. With that figured, telling the north-south directions become easy.

During the night, a little knowledge of astronomy will go a long way. The aim is to find the North star. To do that, find the Big Dipper, which is one of the clearest constellations in the northern night sky; it looks like a ladle. Following the front edge of its 'cup' from bottom to top, if you extend that line five times up, you will see a star. That's the North star.

If this sounds too complicated, then try this: If the moon is in the crescent phase, imagine a line running from its tip to bottom tip and continuing all the way down to the horizon. If you're in the northern hemisphere, the point where the imaginary line touches the ground is the south.

Telling time without a watch

Extend your hand out from your shoulder and count the number of hand's breadth from the horizon up to the sun. Each finger is about fifteen minutes and each hand's breadth is an hour. And that's the number of hours till sunset.

You could alternately try making the universal drinking sign, put your little finger down on the horizon and count the hand breadths all the way to the same. Each hand's breadth is an hour.

It won't be precise, but it will be very helpful in case of an emergency.

Starting a fire without matches or a lighter

Try to carry a lighter and a few birthday candles but if you have neither, try these methods.

- If you are carrying a plastic water bottle with a convex curvature, you can angle it right in front of the sun and focus down the sun's rays like a magnifying glass on dry tinder and make a flame. The plastic bottle can be replaced by a ziplock pouch filled with water. The technique remains the same. All you need is the sun overhead and really dry tinder.

- You could go with the age-old method of rubbing sticks together vigorously until they produce smoke. This will take a while. Then add dry grass to it, blow air on it gently until it combusts into flames. If you can't find anything flammable, use the lint on your socks. Cotton and wool are flammable materials so if you're wearing either cotton or woollen socks, you can pluck off loose strands and fibres for a tinder pile and add it to the smoking wood.
- A faster way to create friction fire is to use your knife and make small holes in a flat piece of soft dry wood (like a hearth board) and use a spindle-like stick to rub down into that hole in a strong circular motion. Once the hole is ready, set a small wood chip under it and start rubbing the spindle hard, with a lot of pressure. Soon it will start to smoke up. Add the smoking wood chip to a pile of dry grass and cover it with the grass nest. Gently blow on it, until thick smoke starts to come out. Within minutes, the dry grass 'nest' will turn into a proper fire.
- You could also use a silver foil wrapper of a Kitkat chocolate and a small A1 battery. Read about this brilliant trick online. It does work!

(It is important to use these methods responsibly so as not to set off a jungle fire.)

Surviving insects and bugs in the wild

Clothing is the first line of defence outdoors. In hot weather, wearing lightweight, tightly woven pants and full sleeves shirts provide some amount of protection. But if it's not too hot, clothing made from stronger, thicker fabrics is a good way to protect against insect bites. Add a fine mesh bug-repelling headnet over your hat and you're set. You might look ridiculous, but it'll protect the entire head area from smaller insects. Wear long socks and tuck your pants into your socks! If you can wear gloves that insects can't bite through, even better. (Yes, you'll probably look ludicrous, but it'll save you from serious bites, leeches and ensuing illnesses.)

Importantly, wear light-coloured clothing as they attract less bugs than the dark ones.

Carry a good-quality insect repellent cream or spray. Use the deet-free ones on the skin and the deet repellent on your clothing. Slather it on the areas where insects/bugs are most likely to enter your clothing, for example, the waist, ankles, wrists and neck areas. Also buy smoke sticks and candles but try not to inhale them.

If there are pines in the wild and mosquitoes are a concern, then crush a bunch of pine needles in your hands and rub them on your clothes and exposed skin. They work as excellent repellents.

Removing a leech and cleaning the wound

Slide your fingernail under the sucker. Use one hand to gently pull the skin near the sucker, then place your other hand next to the leech and slide one of your fingernails underneath it. The leech will immediately begin attempting to reattach itself, so flick it off right away. Do not yank off the leech, since this will leave its sucker attached to your body. Treat the open wound. When you remove a leech, it might bleed for several hours or even days before the anticoagulant leaves your system. Be prepared for the sight of profuse bleeding when you take the leech off. Cleanse the open wound with rubbing alcohol or another first-aid cleansing solution, then apply a bandage to protect it. Since the bleeding might take a while to stop, the bandage will need to be changed regularly. It's important to treat the area as you would any open wound, especially if you're hiking around in a jungle. Open wounds are more susceptible to getting infected in jungle environments. Expect the wound to itch while it heals.

Avoid removing leeches by any other means. It is often suggested that a leech can be removed by pouring salt on it, burning it, spraying it with repellent or drowning it in shampoo. While these techniques might cause the leech to release its grip and fall off, it won't do so before vomiting back into the wound. This can lead to bad infections, so stick to simply using a fingernail or other straight edge to get under the sucker. Get treated immediately if you show signs of a leech allergy. Few people are allergic to leeches, but it does happen. If you experience dizziness, a rash, shortness of breath or swelling, take an antihistamine and seek medical attention right away.

Surviving in the face of a predator

Now the survival technique depends on who or what the predator is! One size doesn't fit all! Read up on the animals in the area online beforehand and listen to the experts. I cannot take any kind of responsibility if you mix things up and decide to fight back a grizzly bear or play dead when faced by the black one!

ACKNOWLEDGEMENTS

AS JOHN DONNE RIGHTLY SAID, 'NO MAN IS AN ISLAND'. AND no literary journey is possible or worthwhile without the love and support of family and friends. I have had many strong allies while penning this account and for that, I am deeply grateful.

I would like to start by thanking my incredible parents for giving me wings and being my greatest strength. My gritty and wise beyond her years sister, Neha, for unwittingly becoming my partner-in-crime through countless adventures and childhood misdemeanours. There have been many. And you never told on me!

I also want to thank Rajdeep Mukherjee and Prasun Chatterjee of Pan Macmillan India, who saw the merit in sharing this tale with the world. My special thanks to Teesta Guha Sarkar for her support, Isha Banerji for her diligence as the editor and a big thank-you to my wonderful literary agent, Sherna Khambatta, who found the perfect home for this story.

I also want to acknowledge the great institution of the Indian Armed Forces, which my father served proudly, for giving me the kind of life skills that have set me up for life.

And Tawang, for giving me my greatest adventure yet …

ABOUT THE AUTHOR

Nidhie Sharma is a writer–director and the author of *Dancing with Demons*, India's first work of fiction on boxing. She studied filmmaking and screenwriting at New York University and New York Film Academy, before which she graduated with honours in English Literature. Nidhie was raised in an armed forces environment and has travelled extensively across the world. *Invictus* chronicles a real-life event from her childhood. Nidhie lives in Mumbai. She is on Twitter and Instagram as @iamnidhiesharma.